D1478981

PEKING OPERA
AND
MEI LANFANG

A Guide to China's Traditional Theatre
And the Art of Its Great Master

By Wu Zuguang, Huang Zuolin and Mei Shaowu

With Selections from Mei Lanfang's Own Writings

NEW WORLD PRESS
BEIJING, CHINA

First Edition   1980

Second Printing   1984

Published by the New World Press
24 Baiwanzhuang Road, Beijing, China

Printed by the Foreign Languages Printing House
19 Chegongzhuang Road, Beijing, China

Distributed by China International Book Trading Corporation
(Guoji Shudian)
P.O. Box 399, Beijing, China

Printed in the People's Republic of China

CONTENTS

LIST OF ILLUSTRATIONS

PLATES

LINE DRAWINGS IN TEXT

All line drawings were done by Sun Chengwu

FOREWORD

Many theatre-goers abroad are interested in Peking Opera, the popular traditional theatre of China, and find it both exotic and fascinating. Half a century ago, describing his first experience in watching a Peking Opera performance given by the great stage artist Mei Lanfang and his company then touring the United States, an American critic wrote:

> You will be puzzled all the way through, and a little bored once in a while; but in spite of knowing nothing of the dramatic background (of Peking Opera), in spite of hundreds of rigid conventions of staging and gesture, in spite of the musical accompaniment that often outrages your ears, you will be charmed and fascinated and now and then swept quite off your feet.

Today, even though there are many more Peking Opera troupes going abroad than in the thirties, that American critic's experience may still be shared by those who watch a Peking Opera show for the first time. But after attending more performances, he perhaps will be able to comprehend the mass of intricate conventions of this classical theatre, appreciate its unique artistry and enjoy not only the acting and acrobatics but also its music, singing and recitations. The purpose of this book is to familiarize interested theatre-goers and readers with all the distinctive characteristics of Peking Opera and provide them with background information necessary for total enjoyment.

Since Mei Lanfang was the first Chinese artist to introduce Peking Opera to audiences abroad and contribute to its great popularity, the book treats the art of Peking Opera mainly as it was interpreted by Mei Lanfang. It includes among its authors accomplished writers in this field, who have an intimate knowledge of both Peking Opera and the great master. It also includes comments by many authoritative foreign critics on the art of Peking Opera as exhibited in the performances of Mei Lanfang.

While it is hoped that the book will appeal to the general reader as a guide to Peking Opera, it is also intended for those who wish to go deeper into the subject. The selections from Mei Lanfang's own writings and a comparative study of Mei Lanfang, Stanislavsky and Brecht by the dramatist Huang Zuolin will prove of particular interest to students of the Chinese theatre.

Many people have helped us in preparing the book. We should like to thank especially Mr. Xu Jichuan, a close friend of Mei Lanfang, and the Research Institute of Traditional Chinese Drama for their valuable suggestions.

— Editors

PEKING OPERA AND ITS GREAT
MASTER MEI LANFANG

Wu Zuguang

For more than half a century, the name of Peking Opera has
been associated with that of Mei Lanfang (1894-1961), a renowned impersonator of the female role. Peking Opera, a major
Chinese theatrical form, enjoys great popularity both at home
and abroad. To many foreign theatre-goers, it is almost synon-
ymous with China's classical theatre. Mei Lanfang was a great
exponent of this traditional art. He was the first to introduce
Peking Opera to foreign audiences and made highly successful
tours of Japan (1919, 1924 and 1956), the United States (1930)
and the Soviet Union (1935). His superb and enchanting performances brought out the best in Peking Opera and classical Chinese dramatic art in general. He was a true ambassador in art.

I shall first deal with various features of Peking Opera as an
art and then go on to elaborate the contributions made to it by
Mei Lanfang.

PEKING OPERA — A COMPREHENSIVE ART FORM

Peking Opera is the most representative of all Chinese traditional dramatic art forms. Created and developed by talented
artists over a period of several centuries, classical Chinese
drama is a comprehensive performing art with a unique form of

Wu Zuguang is a well-known playwright and dramatic critic.

its own — comprehensive because it is an ingenious combination of elements from many sources: traditional Chinese music, poetry, singing, recitation, dancing, acrobatics and martial skills, all blended into one great theatrical art without a trace of affectation.

Varying in style from place to place, the traditional theatre in our vast, populous country boasts over a hundred different types, with singing as their common feature. Hence, traditional Chinese drama is a kind of singing drama or opera and yet it has nothing in common with the opera or operetta of the West. It is much more than mere opera or operetta in the usual sense.

THE ORIGIN OF PEKING OPERA

Each of the 100-odd types of traditional Chinese drama employs the dialect of a particular locality, with a particular musical style and repertory typical of that area. Otherwise, in costuming, make-up and the style of acting, they are more or less the same, except that some are more refined while others are less polished or even crude. Peking Opera, so named because it was a new theatrical form evolved from several types of local operas being staged in Beijing (Peking) some 200 years ago, is just one of these 100-odd local operas. Patronized by men of letters, artists, audiences from all walks of life, the Qing Court (which held sway from 1644 until 1911) and post-Qing officialdom, it was steadily developed and improved by masters of performing art for many generations before it reached maturity and perfection. It is considered a superb art form famous for its great artistic skill in singing, dancing and martial skills.

Theatrical art forms in many countries do not present singing, dancing and spoken parts in one single drama. An opera singer, for instance, neither dances nor speaks on stage; there are no singing or dancing parts in a modern play; in a dance drama the dancer has no speaking role and does not sing either. Traditional Chinese drama, including Peking Opera, as described above, is a kind of entertainment which includes spoken parts, singing, dancing and acrobatics. These demands call for versatility on the part of the performers, particularly those of Peking

Opera. An all-round top-notch Peking Opera performer, for instance, must be good-looking or attractive when appearing in make-up, of pleasing physical proportions, with a pair of expressive eyes and a rich variety of facial expression. Whether of the warrior type or not, an actor must undergo years of fundamental training in martial skills so that every movement on the stage is gracefully and precisely made and every pose assumed at the end of a movement makes the performer resemble a piece of well executed sculpture, thereby increasing the aesthetic value of the acting.

A performer from a regular, professional Peking Opera troupe is required to undergo at least seven or eight — sometimes as many as a dozen — years of such basic training, after which he must still keep on practising all aspects of the art, including singing and recitation, for the rest of his working life.

SYMBOLISM IN ACTING

Acting in Peking Opera is not subjected to the limitations of time and space; here symbolism is essential. Since some activities in everyday life cannot possibly be reproduced on the stage, Peking Opera gives expression to them in a symbolic way. Thus, particular bodily movements signify opening or closing a door, entering or leaving a room, going upstairs or down, climbing a mountain or wading across a stream. Circling the stage, whip in hand, suggests riding a horse; riding in a carriage is represented by an attendant holding flags painted with a wheel design on either side of the performer; walking in a circle indicates a long journey; four soldiers and four generals flanking both sides of the stage represent an army several thousand strong; two men somersaulting under a spotlight shows the audience how they are groping and fighting in the dark; and on a stage bare of scenery, a performer holding an oar or paddle and doing knee-bends to simulate a heavy swell, demonstrates travelling on a boat.... The scenery used in modern theatre is out of place on the Peking Opera stage, because it would only serve to restrict the performers' acting. The setting is created entirely by a performer's acting which mentally brings the audience to any place where the story of the drama takes place. Thus, the scene could be a vast open plain with birds flying in the sky or broad expanse of water with fish swimming about; all this is projected on to the stage through the mind's eye of the audience. There is a saying: "Small as the stage is, a few steps will bring you far beyond heaven." The actions on the stage are stylized dance-like movements accompanied by singing, dialogues and instrumental music. It is through these highly abstract but meaningful modes of expression — we might call them symbolic — that the audience is led to an understanding of what is taking place on the stage. These actions carry the audience on wings of imagination to perception of the true environment of the play. The stage effect is, in a sense, even more powerful than that produced by scenery, backdrops and properties.

MUSIC, DIALOGUE AND SONG

The wind, stringed and percussion instruments are all used in Peking Opera music. The main percussion instruments are gongs and drums of various sizes and shapes. There are also clappers made of hard wood or bamboo. With these percussion instruments, which may sound rather monotonous, a very strong rhythmical effect is nevertheless produced. A really good drummer (he is also the conductor), using an implement like a pair of chopsticks, is able to create a very powerful sound effect — sometimes loud, sometimes soft, sometimes strong and exciting, sometimes faint and sentimental — to bring out the emotions of the characters in coordination with the acting of the performers.

The main stringed instrument used is the fiddle known as the *jing hu* (Beijing fiddle) supported by an *er hu* (second fiddle). The plucked stringed instruments in use include the *yue qin* (the moon-shaped mandolin), the *pi pa* (a four-stringed lute) and *xian zi* (a three-stringed lute). Occasionally, the *suo na* horn and Chinese flute are also used. They played in unison, which is characteristic of Oriental music.

The vocal part of Peking Opera consists of both spoken and singing parts. The spoken parts are again subdivided into the "rhyme" part (recitation with rhythms and rhymes) and the "Beijing dialect" part. The rhyme part has an accent close to that of the dialects of Hubei and Anhui provinces. The Beijing dialect part, also with rhymes, is closer to the colloquial language spoken in Beijing. Generally, the former is used in historical and full-length operas while the latter is used in folk operettas; the positive and serious characters use the former while the latter is used by clowns, frivolous female roles and children's parts.

The musical modes in Peking Opera consist mainly of *er huang* and *xi pi*. *Er huang* is adapted from the folk tunes of Anhui and Hubei while *xi pi* stems from the tunes of Shaanxi Province in northwest China. The melodies, set to different lyrics, are each designed on a fixed pattern. In addition, Peking Opera music also assimilates the lyrics of the musical system of the much older *kun qu* opera of the south and some folk arias popular in the north. These different tunes and lyrics, in specific programmes, are so harmoniously arranged that they give effect and support to actions taking place on the stage.

DIFFERENT TYPES OF ROLES

Peking Opera roles are classified according to the age and personality of the characters. All female roles are known as *dan,* which is subdivided into *qing yi* (the quiet and gentle), *hua dan* (the vivacious or dissolute type), *wu dan* (women with martial skills), *dao ma dan* (sword and horse type, women skilled in fighting with weapons) and *lao dan* (old woman). All male roles are called *sheng,* which is subdivided into *lao sheng* (old man), *xiao sheng* (young man) and *wu sheng* (the warrior type). The third role-type, known as *jing* (the painted-face), portrays either people who are frank and open-minded but rough, or those who are crafty and dangerous. These are again subdivided into the principal painted-face and the minor painted-face, the civilian painted-face and the warrior painted-face. Some *jing* roles are devoted more to singing while others stress acting. The audience is able to distinguish the loyal from the treacherous, the good from the wicked by studying the make-up and costumes. *Chou*, a clown, is depicted by a dab of white on the face. He is funny and humorous. This role is again sub-divided into "civilian clowns" and "warrior clowns".

Each of these different role-types has a style and rules of its own. Although all performers sing the tunes of *xi pi* and *er huang*, the talented, past and present, have been able to create their own style of singing and recitation with variations to suit their own voices and thus could bring out even more clearly the sentiments and emotions of the characters they portray.

Some people think that the Peking Opera method of presentation is not true to the "rules" of drama. For instance, they point out, the struggle between the hero and the villain in modern theatre or on the screen is invariably unfolded in a series of actions and the villain will be found out only at the end of the story. By contrast, in Peking Opera, the hero or villain introduces himself to the audience at the very beginning, and is usually recognized without difficulty by the way his face is painted or the costume he wears. Like a modern play or film, Peking Opera has a script. But generally speaking, what attracts the Peking Opera fan is not so much the story itself, which he knows only too well, but the artistic performance of an actor or actress. The Peking Opera fan follows closely the gestures and movements of the players, some scenes of combat on the stage, or listens attentively to certain parts of the singing or recitation in which he is particularly interested. Moreover, he never gets tired of seeing or listening to it, ten or twenty times over. This is also the case with people of the West who go to an opera house to listen to the same opera, or to a theatre to see the same play or ballet over and over again.

MAKE-UP, COSTUMES AND PROPS

Like the other types of traditional drama, Peking Opera was originally a folk art. It has been suggested that its staging in the open air in the early years led to the use of excessively heavy make-up, using heavy paint in bright colours. The most typical style of make-up is the lines and mask-designs on the faces of the *jing* role actors. When applying make-up, the first step is to lift the eyebrows, to give the performer an impressive or dignified appearance.

The costumes are themselves *objets d'art*, based on those of the Ming dynasty (1368-1644). The colour scheme consists of a variety of hues on backgrounds of bright scarlet, bright green, yellow, white, black and purple, embroidered with golden and silver threads to form magnificent, dazzling, brilliant designs. There are very strict rules as to what kind of costume should be worn, depending on the status and personality of the roles being played. The headdress, especially the headgear for *dan* roles, is particularly spectacular. Sometimes, however, for special effect, the plain and elegant headdress for some particular character is in striking contrast to the lavishly embellished headdress of the other characters. The properties, too, are ornamented, modified versions of things used on real life; some of them, even mundane objects like weapons, tables or chairs, lanterns or candlesticks, dishes, bowls, trays and bed curtains, are nevertheless exquisite artifacts. In fact the Peking Opera stage resembles a wonderland full of sparkling, eye-catching spectacles.

MEI LANFANG — THE GREAT MASTER OF PEKING OPERA

Next, about Mei Lanfang as I knew him.

Mei Lanfang started learning Peking Opera at eight years of age and made his *début* on stage as a female role player at eleven. When he died in 1961 at the age of 67, he was looked upon as the great master of Peking Opera. For half a century Mei Lanfang was a household word in this country and, right up to the time of his death, he managed to preserve the splendour of his art, playing the roles with the same vitality as always.

For more than 2,000 years of feudalism, women had to observe a special code of conduct which required them to confine themselves to their living quarters, to say nothing of going on the boards. This is the reason why, throughout the history of Chinese classical theatre, men all along played the female role on stage right up to the close of the Qing dynasty. It was due to this time-honoured tradition that the performing art of the *dan* role played by men developed and flourished. The 1920s and the three decades that followed saw the golden age of the *dan* role in Peking Opera, from which "the four great *dan* (female-role) actors"* emerged, and Mei Lanfang is acknowledged indisputably to have been the best of all.

BORN TO A FAMILY OF ACTORS

Mei Lanfang was born in Beijing into a "Peking Opera family" in 1894. His grandfather Mei Qiaoling (1842-1881) was a famous *dan* role player and the leader of the "Four Happiness Troupe" in Beijing, then one of the four leading troupes originally from Anhui. His father Mei Zhufen (1874-1896) was another outstanding actor and his uncle Mei Yutian (1869-1914) was a talented musician and a famous *jing hu* (Beijing fiddle) player. Mei Baojiu, Mei Lanfang's youngest son, is also an accomplished *dan* player. So the Meis have for four generations performed female roles in Peking Opera, which constitutes quite an interesting episode in the history of the Chinese theatre.

Mei Qiaoling was a gifted, celebrated, creative actor. In the old days, there were rigid divisions between the different *dan* roles: a *qing yi* actor, for instance, was supposed to play only the roles of dignified, graceful females whereas a vivacious, pretty young woman would be played exclusively by a *hua dan* actor belonging to the same troupe. Mei Qiaoling was the first to break away from this age-old convention to become equally accomplished in both role-types. This probably paved the way for his grandson Mei Lanfang to rise as a great master of Peking Opera, first specializing in *qing yi* which is mainly a

---

* Of the four great *dan* (female-role) actors, the three others were Cheng Yanqiu (1904-1958), Shang Xiaoyun (1899-1976) and Xun Huisheng (1899-1968).

singing role. Later on, he became skilled in playing the other types of female role, namely, the *gui men dan* (unmarried young girl) and *hua dan* (woman of the vivacious type) and also *dao ma dan* (woman warrior). As an all-around female role player, he thus enriched the performing art in this field.

Mei Lanfang won national fame before he was twenty. In lines dedicated to Mei Lanfang, one of his contemporaries, a poet, wrote:

> *A smile brings an eternal spring,*
> *And a sob unending sorrows.*

BOTH SUCCESSOR AND PIONEER

As the doyen of traditional Chinese theatre, he was successor to and pioneer of *dan* roles in Peking Opera, for it was he who inherited and systematically studied the fine tradition of his predecessors, and at the same time developed and gave greater scope to their artistic endeavour. Since singing, dancing and acting are the three main components of traditional Chinese drama, he became highly accomplished in all three, a virtuoso of *qing yi, hua dan* and *dao ma dan*. If his grandfather Mei Qiaoling was the one who made a break from the convention of maintaining rigid divisions between different female role players, and had thus given greater scope to the art of acting the *dan* roles, then it was Mei Lanfang who fulfilled his predecessors' unfinished experiment to turn himself into a performer of multi-female roles, well versed not only in singing but also in dancing and acting as well. After many years of effort he enabled the *dan* role to occupy a very important place in Peking Opera with a clear-cut form for new-comers to follow and develop.

In over 50 years of stage life, Mei Lanfang had played no less than 100 different characters in the traditional Peking Opera repertoire. Thanks to long years of gruelling practice and continued research, he created many lively unforgettable characters on stage. Among them were Zhao Yanrong (in *Beauty Defies*

Tyranny), a sycophant court minister's beautiful daughter who feigns insanity to avoid falling into the hands of the emperor; Lady White (in *The White Snake*), a pretty woman changed by metamorphosis from a snake, in love with a young scholar; Su San (in *Lady Magnolia*), a wronged courtesan on trial before a panel of judges, one of whom happens to be her long-lost lover; and Yang Yuhuan (in *The Drunken Beauty*), the concubine of the Emperor Ming Huang of the Tang dynasty (618-907), who took a drop too much and is known as "the Drunken Beauty". He also created many new plays, making reforms and improvements in both make-up and costumes. They are dramatizations of either historical episodes or classical literary works. The choreography for these new dramas was designed by Mei Lanfang and he also composed new arias for them. These include *The King's Parting with His Favourite, The Goddess of the River Luo,* Beauty Xi Shi* (about a patriotic woman sent to live with the sovereign of an enemy country for the purpose of revenging the ruin of her homeland), *Daiyu Burying Flowers* (an episode from the novel *A Dream of Red Mansions*). He also produced and personally appeared in a number of operas with contemporary themes protesting against the deplorable marital institutions and customs of the old society and against the injustices done to the women under such oppression. For half a century, Mei Lanfang not only won the admiration of his audiences with the charm of his artistic excellence, but also their respect because of his great love for social justice.

The last new item Mei Lanfang produced and added to his repertoire is entitled *Mu Guiying Takes Command,* in which he portrayed the image of the heroine Mu Guiying, already in her middle age, assuming command of an army to fight the aggressors.

---

* The story of *The Goddess of the River Luo* is based on a prose poem written by Cao Zhi (192-232), a famous poet of the Wei State (220-265) during the period of Three Kingdoms. It is a love tale between the poet himself and the Goddess of the River Luo who, in reality, was the shade of his departed loved one.

Mei Qiaoling, Mei Lanfang's grandfather, in the costume of the *dan* (female) role. He was one of the most popular and versatile *dan* actors in the latter half of the 19th century.

Mei Lanfang in 1905 at age 12, the year he made his début on the stage.

Mei Lanfang won national fame before he was twenty.

Mei Lanfang as a woman warrior in *Fanjiang Pass* (1913).

Mei Lanfang as Daiyu in *Daiyu Burying Flowers* (1919).

Mei Lanfang as Xi Shi in *Beauty Xi Shi* (1929).

Mei Lanfang (as Lady White) with Yu Chengfei (as the scholar), a famous *xiao sheng* (young man) actor, and Mei Baojiu (as the maid-servant Blue Snake).

Mei Lanfang as the wronged courtesan Su San with the renowned *chou* (clown) actor Xiao Changhua as the old warder. Su San is telling her sufferings to the kind-hearted warder, who escorted her to the provincial capital for a trial.

Mei Lanfang as Yu Ji and Liu Lianrong as the King of Chu, a distinguished *jing* (painted-face) actor, in *The King's Parting with His Favourite*.

During the Japanese occupation of Shanghai, Mei Lanfang grew a moustache as a form of protest and stopped performing. At this time he managed to earn a living by painting.

Four Great *Dan* (female-role) Actors: Mei Lanfang, Shang Xiaoyun (left), Xun Hui-sheng (right) and Cheng Yanqiu (front).

Talking shop with leading actors and actresses.

Discussing acting techniques with Chen Bohua, a famous Hubei opera actress.

Premier Zhou Enlai chatting with Mei Lanfang.

SECRET OF HIS SUCCESS

Mei Lanfang's childhood was a miserable one. He was orphaned young, losing his father at four and his mother when he was 15. It was his uncle Mei Yutian who brought him up. But Mei Yutian himself was in financial straits, so young Mei Lanfang had to start his career as an actor very early. In retrospect, he wrote:

I was a very dull student of this art. I was not gifted. The need for diligent practice was all that I understood. The way I learned this art was much the same as the training that many others went through. I knew of no short-cuts and never expected to learn things without effort. I have an aversion to flattery. All these decades, I have depended on my teachers and friends who have been outspoken enough to point out my shortcomings so that I could correct them in time. . . .

According to another account, he said he never was an actor with great natural endowments. He had, for instance, a pair of lack-lustre eyes when he was a child. To remedy this, he exercised his eyes relentlessly. He would practise gazing at the movements of an incense flame in a dark room; fly kites and stare at them drifting in a blue sky; keep pigeons in order to look at them soaring higher and higher until they disappeared into the clouds. . . . These were some of the ways in which he managed to give himself a pair of bright, keen, highly expressive eyes.

Mei Lanfang was a conscientious student, always showing a strong desire to learn. He made friends with many distinguished scholars, artists and other personages both at home and abroad. He took the time and trouble to learn Chinese traditional painting and calligraphy from Qi Baishi (1863-1957) and other eminent painters. He made an extensive collection of ancient manuscripts and old treatises on classical music and dance. His intimate knowledge of these partly accounted for the success with which he introduced innovations into the music and dancing of Peking

Opera. During his performance tours of the United States, the Soviet Union and Japan, he had the chance to meet Charles Chaplin, Paul Robeson, Konstantin Stanislavsky and Ichikawa and became their great friends. In these overseas tours he undertook to project the art of traditional Chinese drama to the outside world and at the same time broaden his own vision in the field of art.

He owed his achievements to his life-long habit of hard work. In his autobiography *Forty Years on Stage* he recalled how he persisted in rigorous and regular training all his life, which made a gruelling daily routine. He believed that one must learn to tackle the more difficult jobs in life first and that the sweetness of a thing comes only after one has tasted the bitterness of effort and sweating. "I am now sixty," he once recalled, "but I am still fit to play *dao ma dan* (woman warrior) roles on the stage, like characters in *The Drunken Beauty, Mu's Village Fortress* * and *Rainbow Pass*. This I attribute to the rigid basic training programme my teacher drew up for me, and to which I faithfully adhered."

The secret of his success lay in his painstaking and uninterrupted practice, his acceptance of the critical opinions of others and his own severe criticism of himself. Indeed, this is the path to success for any person.

ATTRACTIVE PERSONALITY

Anyone who knew Mei Lanfang was impressed by his personality and the way he conducted himself. He was a gentlehearted, modest, quiet man who respected both himself and others. Like the gentle and upright characters he portrayed on the stage, he retained these qualities all his life, and they were an integral part of his attractive personality.

Another sterling quality of Mei Lanfang's that commanded our respect was his patriotism and moral integrity. China

---

* *Mu's Village Fortress* tells about the love story of the young heroine Mu Guiying.

had a history of great suffering in the long past, so much so that the qualities of gentility and goodness had almost become euphemisms for cowardice and timidity. But it was during the eight years of Japanese aggression (1937-1945) against his country that this otherwise gentle and good-natured Mei Lanfang defied the enemy by growing a moustache to keep himself away from the stage when he had to live in enemy-occupied Shanghai. With great firmness and courage, he coped with all kinds of harassments. He pawned and sold his belongings to support his family and impoverished friends in the same profession and managed to earn a living by painting. He retired from the stage for precisely the eight long years of Japanese occupation without bowing to the wishes of the enemy. As a great artist, he knew what to love and what to hate.

MEI LANFANG, STANISLAVSKY, BRECHT — A STUDY IN CONTRASTS

Huang Zuolin

A dramatic artist, like other artists using other devices, uses theatrical means to reflect life and to influence it. Just as men's views on life and art are conditioned and limited by the particular historical period and class society to which they happen to belong, so dramatic methods vary from age to age, subject as a rule to the dictates of time and class, though this is not necessarily always so.

ENDLESS SEARCH FOR NEW THEATRICAL TRUTHS

The history of the theatre is a summary of man's endless search for new dramatic means of expression and new theatrical truths. The valuable experiences have been preserved and the worthless ones discarded. In the 25 centuries of the theatre's history, innumerable dramatic methods have come into being; theatre workers in each historical period have sought the best forms possible to convey a definite ideological and political content. The ancient Greeks had their way of expressing the idea of "fate", and when man's will came into conflict with fate dramatists had to introduce the *deus ex machina* to solve life's contradictions to which men at that time were incapable of finding solutions. The miracle and morality plays of the Middle Ages, with their angels and devils, demanded different methods

Huang Zuolin is a noted stage and film director and vice-president of the Chinese Dramatists' Association.

of presentation, while Shakespeare had to resort to the "dynamic use of space" to give full expression to the outbursts of the men of the Renaissance Period. The 17th century Baroque school used a flamboyant and superficial style to put forward the reactionary ideas of absolute monarchy and pander to the tastes of the nobility. The Romantic theatre of the late 18th century devoted itself so exclusively to the importance of the individual spirit that it became divorced from real life and declined into stereo-typed formalism. Thus each age has had its own dramatic techniques and after a long process of evolution the best have been retained and have formed a part of the precious heritage handed down from generation to generation. When such a heritage grows into a system, a school of theatre is born, and it is distinct and complete in itself.

For the sake of discussion, I would like to take three divergent views on the theatre, those of Mei Lanfang, Stanislavsky and Brecht, in order to discover their common features as well as their basic differences. I wish to explore the possibilities re-sulting from the influences one may exert on the other and see if anything new may or will emerge from the old.

SALIENT FEATURES OF TRADITIONAL CHINESE THEATRE

Mei Lanfang, Stanislavsky and Brecht are three great masters of realism, yet each has his own ways and methods of expression. Mei Lanfang was the most representative and mature exponent of the traditional Chinese theatre, a theatre vastly different — indeed, fundamentally different — from that of the West. To my mind, the traditional Chinese theatre at its best has the following salient features:

1. Fluidity: there is no lowering and raising of the curtain or change of scenery as is usually the case on the modern Western stage; instead, the scenes follow straight on one after another. It is an art that always has the appropriate tempo, rhythm and montage;

2.   Plasticity: the Chinese stage is highly flexible, with no limitations either of time or space;

3.   Sculpturality: whereas the characters on the Western stage are two-dimensional being enclosed, as it were, in a picture frame, those on the traditional Chinese stage stand out three-dimensionally;

4.   Conventionality: the adherence to an elaborate system of commonly recognized conventions is a basic characteristic of the Chinese theatre. We consider it impossible, if not distasteful, to present life, as it is, on the stage without any embellishments. A play is a play; it is frankly theatrical. For this, we have created a set of conventions to break through the limitations of time and space so that life may appear more free and sublime on the stage.

The greatness of Mei Lanfang's art lies in the fact that he brought these four characteristics to perfection. After seeing one of Mei Lanfang's performances, Brecht was full of enthusiasm and praise and he wrote:

> This way of acting is healthier and (in our opinion) worthier of a rational being; it demands considerable experience of life and knowledge of mankind and an acute understanding of social values. Naturally, here too a creative process is at work; but its value is higher, because it has been transmuted to the plane of the conscious.

BRECHT'S THEORY OF DRAMA IN CONTRAST TO STANISLAVSKY'S

The most fundamental thing in Brecht's theory of drama was his conviction that a certain distance must be maintained between the actors and the characters played, between the audience and the actors, and between the audience and the characters. In other words, the actors are not to identify themselves with the characters, neither is the audience to identify itself with the actors, much less with the stage characters. Players, characters and spectators should keep a certain distance from each other.

Thus Brecht wrote, "Not for a second is the actor permitted to identify himself with the character he portrays." This is the complete reverse of Stanislavsky's theory that an actor should "enter into the character". As Sadovsky, one of Stanislavsky's pupils, aptly put it: "Between the actor and the role, there should not be a gap large enough for a needle." Not so Brecht. The reason why he aimed at "distancing" was that he wanted to prevent the theatre from becoming a place of magic enchantment, of "intoxicating, hypnotic effects", to keep the actors from sweeping the audience off their feet so that, in a trance-like state, they identify themselves with the characters in the play and thereby lose what is being presented to them. He used many devices to prevent this state of hallucination, fearful lest actors and spectators carried away by passion should lose their reasoning power and be unable to grasp the dramatist's message soberly and critically, to examine the essence of things. In other words, if the actors or audience were too involved in the plot of the play and the sentiments of the characters, they would not be able to make the best use of their reasoning faculty, their detached scientific judgement, and therefore they would not be in a position to see clearly the life and reality contained in the play, much less transform them.

Brecht has been accused of not wanting actors to show any emotion and only letting them preach dry, didactic sermons. It should be pointed out that this is not the case. He was only opposed to the use of emotion to induce a trance-like state, for he believed that the theatre should open men's minds with reason. His friend, the well-known critic Eric Bentley, once said that Brecht wanted everybody to "think with one's heart, to feel with one's mind". Brecht himself wrote, "It is impossible to explain Epic Drama in a few technical terms. The basic thing, perhaps, is that the Epic Drama does not stimulate the spectators' passion but their intellect." Again he said somewhere, "True emotion is born in the process of feeling and apprehending, and this is exactly what we are after." As I understand it, what he meant was that when reason is sufficiently stimulated it would turn into emotion. And herein should lie the moving power of art. An artist should master emotion, but he should not be mastered by it. A dialectical theatre combining intellect with feeling should be sought, asserted Brecht.

COMMON FEATURES OF THREE GREAT MASTERS OF REALISM

Was Brecht, then, opposed to Stanislavsky? Yes and no, because their views on art were, broadly speaking, identical while their views on the theatre were diametrically opposed. In Brecht and Stanislavsky we find much in common; both of them, for instance, were realists and strong opponents of naturalism. Stanislavsky has often been pronounced guilty of naturalism, when actually this is not the case. In *My Life in Art* he wrote: "Writers of reportage, to raise a laugh, insist that we keep mosquitoes, flies, crickets and other insects . . . and that we force our trained crickets to sing to create an atmosphere true to life on the stage." From this we can see that although Stanislavsky believed in presenting real life on the stage, he certainly did not mean to show life as it is without retouching it. Another similarity between Brecht and Stanislavsky was the stress that both of them laid on stage movement. "The actor," said Brecht, "must find . . . adequate movements to express the emotions of the character he is playing so as best to reveal his mental state. Only when all emotions are brought out and find expression can there be form and meaning." And Stanislavsky said, "The human form — that is the form of his movements. On the stage we must have movement; movement, action — this is the basis of acting. . . . What is invisible must be made visible. . . . More than any other schools, actors of our school must not only pay more attention to the inner organs which produce the process of understanding, but also to the external organs . . . which correctly express emotion." On this point, these great masters of theatre art, Brecht, Stanislavsky and Mei Lanfang, agreed, as another great Chinese actor, Zhang Decheng (1886-1967), the veteran exponent of Sichuan Opera, testified in his well-known saying: "Feeling aroused within finds expression without — in movements and gestures."

THE MOST BASIC DIFFERENCE

So much for common features of Mei Lanfang, Stanislavsky and Brecht. What then are their differences? Put simply, the most basic difference is that Stanislavsky believed in the "fourth wall", Brecht wanted to demolish it, while for Mei Lanfang such a wall did not exist and so there was never any need to pull it down, since the Chinese theatre has always been so highly conventionalized that it has never set out to create an illusion of real life for the audience. In the theatre, the term "fourth wall" is fairly well-known, but probably few people inquire into its origin or comprehend fully its significance in dramatic theory and the far-reaching effect it has had on modern stage-craft. This term was coined 93 years ago, on March 30, 1887, to be exact, at a time when the theatre in the West was in a very bad way, empty, artificial, piteously devoid of life and content. This was what Zola called "the mouldering ruins of yesterday's theatre". And Mérimée summed up the French drama of this period in the formula: "Pan, pan, pan. The three raps. Curtain rises. Smile, suffer, weep, kill. He is killed, she is dead. Finis." To break through this old formula, Zola and his contemporaries clamoured with one voice that "the theatre must be saved", and the panacea they proposed was Science. For science at that time was the moving force even in the world of letters, and nothing could be established unless it had undergone scientific tests. Moreover, after the French bourgeois revolution and the Paris Commune, the people had lost interest in plays about high-born society and the individual soul, and were eagerly demanding plays reflecting ordinary life and their own harsh struggles. The dramatists, starting from the premise that in order to change life they must first be aware of it, began to present real life faithfully, though mechanically, on the stage, just as it was, and called this "scientific". This was how the nat-

uralistic school came into being. Its main protagonist was
André Antoine, who started the Theatre Libre on March 30,
1887. Another playwright, Jean Jullien, spokesman of this
school, declared almost on the same day, "The actor must perform as if he were at home, without worrying about the audience's reaction. Whether the spectators applaud or condemn
him has nothing to do with him. There must be a fourth wall
before the stage, a wall transparent for the audience,
opaque for the actor." And this led to Stanislavsky's principle of "public isolation from the audience". After André Antoine and his group erected this wall separating the actor from
the audience, the theatre took on a new lease of life and many
fine works appeared, for the naturalistic drama produced plays
of critical realism which thoroughly exposed the sordid nature
of bourgeois society with all its vices, follies and hypocrisy.
Outstanding 19th century playwrights of this school included
Ibsen, Bernard Shaw, Hauptmann, Chekhov and others. The
modern Chinese drama, as we all know, also had its birth during the heyday of this school and has in the course of the past
seven decades served its purpose and won its rightful place in
the hearts of the people.

I would like to call attention to one question here. This
mode of expression, this attempt to create a fourth wall, an
illusion of real life on the stage, is only one of many devices
in the theatre. In the 2,500 years of dramatic development
this method has a history of 93 years only, and even during this
brief period not all playwrights have used it. Its influence has
been so great, however, that some people seem to regard it as
the only technique. This imposes limitations, restricting us by
the framework of the stage, and thereby seriously hampering
creativeness. In order to break through this restriction, Brecht
proposed to pull down the fourth wall and dispel the illusion of
real life. In its place he employed the *Verfremdungseffekt*
(effect of "alienation") to shatter the illusion of real life and
prevent the audience from identifying themselves with either
the actors or the characters. Brecht made this comment on the
Stanislavsky school:

Transmutation (of the actor into the character played) is a very tricky business. Stanislavsky prescribed many methods, a whole new system, to produce original feeling in each performance. But an actor cannot enter into his part for long, he is soon exhausted and then he starts to imitate some superficial characteristics of his role, some gesture or intonation, till the effect on the audience is pitifully weakened.

Brecht went on to say:

These difficulties would not beset an actor of the traditional Chinese drama. For from the start he has no idea of transmuting. From beginning to end he simply "quotes" from his character — and how artistically he does it. Apart from one or two comedians, what actor in the West can compare with Mei Lanfang who in ordinary clothes, in a common sitting-room packed with experts and critics, performs without the benefit of make-up or stage lighting and holds his audience spellbound.

These words were written 45 years ago.

AN APPRECIATION OF MEI LANFANG'S ART

In 1935, during Mei Lanfang's visit to the Soviet Union, Brecht had fled from Hitler's persecution to live as a political refugee in Moscow. He was so impressed by Mei Lanfang's art that in 1936 he wrote an article *Verfremdungseffekte in der chinesischen Schauspielkunst*, in which he spoke rapturously of Mei Lanfang and the Chinese theatre, pointing out enthusiastically that what he had been groping for in vain for years had been raised to a very high artistic level by Mei Lanfang. He enjoyed above all Mei Lanfang's performance in *The Fisherman's Revenge*. That article described it in detail, giving warm praise to Mei Lanfang's movements and gestures, especially to his use of the oar, a simple device to denote boating, meandering rivers and all.

A young woman, the daughter of a fisherman, is shown standing and rowing an imaginary boat. To steer it, she uses an oar which barely reaches to her knees. The current becomes faster; she finds it more difficult to keep her balance. Then the boat turns into a creek, and she rows more quietly. Now that is the way to row a boat; but this sequence has something pictorial about it, as if it had been sung in many a ballad and was common knowledge. Each of this girl's movements is as familiar as a picture; each bend of the river is a well-known adventure; even the next bend of the river is known before it comes. This feeling is produced in the audience by the manner in which the actress plays the scene; it is she who makes the occasion seem so memorable.

This reminds me of an incident when *Othello* was staged in Moscow by Stanislavsky at about the same time. His notes as director show how he dealt with the Venetian gondola. Wheels thickly encased in rubber were fitted under the gondola to enable it to move smoothly. . . . Following the example of the two ships in *The Flying Dutchman,* the gondola was pushed by twelve men and sacking blown by fans was used to make waves. . . . Stanislavsky gave detailed instructions regarding the oars, which were made of tin hollowed out inside and half filled with water, to reproduce the sound of splashing so typical of Venice. Thus in the handling of the boat in *Othello* an attempt at verisimilitude was made, while in the Chinese drama *The Fisherman's Revenge* a technique to dispel this illusion was employed.

However, Stanislavsky also admired Mei Lanfang's performance, describing Chinese dramatic art as "the art of regulated and yet free movements". At the same time, Mei Lanfang did not rely entirely on external technique but, like Stanislavsky himself, paid serious attention to the interpretation of inner feelings also. That this is true is brought out by the following anecdote. A famous actress in Peking Opera studied under Mei Lanfang and learned from him one of his favourite roles, the Goddess Luo in *The Goddess of the River Luo.* When she performed, her audience praised her accomplishment and agreed unanimously that she had imitated her master faithfully,

Mei Lanfang as the fisherman's daughter in *The Fisherman's Revenge*.

Mei Lanfang in scene from *The Fisherman's Revenge*, showing the rowing of an imaginary boat.

Mei Lanfang as Goddess Luo in *The Goddess of River Luo*.

A scene from *Beauty Defies Tyranny*. Mei Lanfang portrays the daughter who feigned madness in front of her father with the help of her dumb maid.

Mei Lanfang as Lady Yang
in the *Drunken Beauty*.

Mei Lanfang as Mu Guiying in *Mu Guiying Takes Command*.

copying every gesture and intonation of his, to the minutest detail. One critic pointed out, however, that there was one thing which she evidently lacked, and that was, in her portrayal of the goddess, she ran short of that sylph-like quality which Mei had rendered with such charm. This remark so distressed our conscientious actress that she went and sought advice everywhere: how was this sylph-like quality to be achieved? One day a connoisseur told her the crux of the matter, "Mei Lanfang played the part of the goddess, while you played the part of Mei Lanfang." Then she began to see the light. This example shows that inner creativeness rather than external manifestations is the true essence of Chinese theatrical art.

DIFFERENT DRAMATIC CONCEPTS AND METHODS

I have tried to show the dialectical relationship between Mei Lanfang, Stanislavsky and Brecht. Their views on art in general agree more or less, but not their views on the theatre. Let us approach this problem from another angle: Some of our theatre workers engaged in the reform of the traditional theatre have paid insufficient attention to different concepts of drama, with the result that they have tended to force Western dramatic techniques on to traditional drama, producing something incongruous. A playwright should go deep into life, but this does not mean that we can bring real life as it is, unmodified, on to the stage. Mao Zedong said that art "ought to be on a higher plane, more intense, more concentrated, more typical, nearer the ideal, and therefore more universal than actual everyday life". And this demand, like other demands made by him, had its mass basis. For the world of actuality and the world of the theatre are not one and the same thing. When our modern drama troupes go to perform "spoken" dramas instead of the traditional operas in the villages, they often come up against an embarrassing situation. The curtain has risen and the play is on, but the peasants still stay outside the hall, smoking or chatting; and when asked to take their seats they would retort, "What's the hurry? The music hasn't started. Those fellows on the stage are just having a chat like ourselves. We will go in when they start to sing."

To sum up, 25 centuries have seen innumerable dramatic methods, but all of these come under two main concepts of the theatre: the theatre to create an illusion of life, and the theatre to dispel that illusion. In other words, drama with realistic staging and drama with conventionalized staging. Apart from these, there may possibly be a third concept combining both modes of expression, realistic and conventional. The school concerned solely with realistic portrayal has a history of only 93 years, and naturalism having fulfilled its historical mission has died a natural death, so to speak. In spite of this, our modern playwrights seem to be fettered by vestiges of this concept. And since the script of a play is the basis of the staged performance, a play written in a realistic manner can hardly be staged in any other fashion without causing a clash between the writer and the producer. But traditional Chinese drama has a technique much more subtle and flexible than the modern stage technique. To take one simple example: By making a character upon his first entrance frankly and openly tell his own story direct to the audience, a more concise and forceful effect is achieved than is often attained in one whole scene in a modern play; while by making a simple "aside", thereby sharing a secret with the audience, a character can lay bare his innermost thoughts.

BRECHT'S ADOPTION OF CHINESE THEATRICAL TECHNIQUES

In the course of his work, Brecht actually adopted a number of techniques from the traditional Chinese theatre. One of these is his method of "quotation". He makes an actor "quote" the character played, like a traditional Chinese story-teller who steps in and out of the role at will, sometimes entering into the part, sometimes making comments in the first person. This shifting of position facilitates the unfolding of the story, the delineation of character and the elucidation of the author's intention. The theory of this method is set forth in Brecht's collection of essays on dramaturgy, *Die Strassenszene*, which presents some of the chief characteristics of the Epic Drama.

Brecht's principle in writing plays was to start with action and then create characters, instead of starting with characters and trying to find suitable actions to bring them out. Another distinctive technique was what he called "the historification of everyday life". Thus he said, "An incident in history happens once and is gone for ever. Every age has its specific characteristics, and everything belonging to that period bears the imprint of the age. Specific historical conditions produce the specific characteristics of an age or its characters." This actually corresponds to Engels' idea of "the typical character in typical circumstances". In a letter to Lassalle, Engels wrote: "The principal characters in fact are representatives of definite classes and tendencies, and hence definite ideas of their time and the motive of their actions are to be found not in trivial individual desires but in the historical stream upon which they are being carried." Brecht's plays reflecting struggle in modern life, like his *Fears and Miseries of the Third Reich,* are good examples drawn from this "Historical Stream".

The "historification of everyday life" is a technique well worth studying. And it will repay us to consider it in conjunction with the following passage from Mao Zedong's *Talks at the Yenan Forum on Literature and Art:*

Revolutionary literature and art should create a variety of characters out of actual life and help the masses to propel history onward. There is, for example, suffering from hunger, cold and oppression, and on the other hand there is exploitation and oppression of man by man. These facts exist everywhere and people look at them as commonplace. When writers and artists concentrate such everyday phenomena, typify the contradictions and struggles within them and produce artistic works, then they can awaken the masses, fire them with enthusiasm and impel them to unite and struggle to transform their environment.

AN INTERESTING QUESTION OF GOOD OR BAD ACTING

Last year I was interviewed by a foreign friend, a fellow theatre worker who asked me a very interesting question. Said he: "A story is current that in a certain city in Italy there was an actor who was famous at playing the villain. Once in *Othello,* he played Iago so well that he aroused so much anger and hatred among the audience that one spectator raised a gun and shot him dead right on the stage. As a token of homage to this famous actor, the city built a fine tomb for him. One day, Stanislavsky happened to pass by and on hearing the story, decided to erect a tombstone in honour of the poor actor with the inscription: "To so-and-so, the best actor in the world." A few years later, Brecht happened to pass by the same place, he too decided to erect a tombstone standing side by side with that of Stanislavsky's with the inscription: "To so-and-so, the worst actor in the world." Now here is the question my foreign friend put to me: "What do you think, sir? Was that actor the best or the worst?" The following is my simple answer: First of all, I was not there when the shooting took place, so I can't pass comment. No investigation, no right to speak. On second thoughts, I think the reason why Stanislavsky held the actor in question in such high esteem was because here actor and character merged into one. Brecht, however, condemned the actor for the same reason, that is, the actor did not hold an objective, critical attitude towards the part so as to let the audience be fully aware of Iago's villainy; instead, so-and-so absorbed the audience in the play to such an extent that they got completely carried away. Experience tells me that after viewing a performance if you hate the character and take a fancy to the actor who portrays it, then the actor is a good one. If the result is to the contrary, then he must be a bad one.

TECHNIQUES OF CHINESE TRADITIONAL ACTING

So, on the question of good acting or bad, we should not be so arbitrary as Stanislavsky or as Brecht. To Mei Lanfang, that is, to the Chinese traditional school of acting, the ideal method is to combine the "inner technique" of introspection with the outgoing techniques of representation. Take Mei Lanfang's performance in *Beauty Defies Tyranny,* in which he played the part of a young woman who feigned madness to tease her father who wanted her to marry the emperor. In this part, he impersonated insanity on the one hand and at the same time remained as sane as the impersonator himself.

Another example is an old play entitled *Writing a Letter to the Southern Tribe* or entitled *Li Bo Composing a Poem While Drunk* in the *kun qu* opera. In this piece, Li Bo, a great poet of the Tang dynasty (618-907), is lying in bed intoxicated when an imperial mandate arrives summoning him to the court at once. An episode in the play depicts him riding a horse in great haste to carry out this order. To depict a drunkard the *cliché* would be to let the actor stagger about on the stage. But not with Chinese traditional acting, for although the poet in the play is drunk, the actor must not forget that he is on horseback. So the two legs do not belong to the poet but to the horse who is not at all drunk. Thereupon, when the great actor Wang Xiaonong (1858-1918) at the turn of the century played the scene, the upper part of his body thoroughly and completely impersonated the drunken poet, but the lower part played the horse, sober and steady. So, may we not say that the upper part is Stanislavskian while the lower part follows Brecht? The dialectical combination of the opposites, sobriety and inebriation, sanity and insanity, is what makes the traditional Chinese theatre so enchanting.

INNER CHARACTERISTICS OF CHINESE THEATRE

As I pointed out at the beginning of this paper, there are four salient characteristics in traditional Chinese theatrical art: fluidity, plasticity, sculpturality and conventionality and the greatest of these being conventionality. But this is not precise enough. To call the traditional Chinese theatre "conventional" is looking at the matter from the view-point of form only; it is not the whole truth. If the keynote to Western art is realism, what then is the essence of traditional Chinese art? It is difficult to find an antonym. In Chinese we have a word for it — *xie yi* — but I have not been able to hit on its English equivalent. When I exchange views with foreign friends on this question, I have to resort to examples from painting. While Western painting is basically realistic, traditional Chinese painting is *"xie yi"*. Take for instance the horses drawn by the Italian artist Giuseppe Castiglione* exhibited at the Palace Museum in Beijing. His horses are as good as real. But take a look at those horses drawn by Xu Beihong (Péon Hsu),** they are over and above the real. Well versed in anatomy, Xu, when he painted, did not go too far away, anatomically speaking, from the real horse, and yet with those few bold touches of his brush, he made his horses not only appear physically true but at the same time he made them seem spiritually alive.

Western critics contrast their own paintings with those of Chinese by saying that while the Western artist takes "the utmost pains to be faithful to what his eye sees; the Chinese artist to what his mind knows". That is to say, the Chinese painter is preoccupied "with the essence rather than the appearance of things". Here I came across this very suggestive word "essence". For short of an apt translation, could we say that realism is the

---

* Giuseppe Castiglione (1688-1766), an Italian Catholic priest, came to Beijing (Peking) in 1715 and was appointed by the Qing emperors as a court painter and artist.

** Xu Beihong (Péon Hsu, 1895-1953) was a distinguished Chinese painter.

keynote of Western art and "essentialism" (*xie yi*) that of Chinese art? If we accept this contrast, the same may be applied to traditional Chinese theatrical art.

By way of summary, besides the four outer characteristics, the traditional Chinese theatre has four inner characteristics:

1. the essentialism of life, i.e., not life as it is, but life as extracted, concentrated and typified. Creative work should not only come out of life but be sublimated, that is, refined from life;

2. the essentialism of movements, i.e., human movements eurythmicized to a higher plane;

3. the essentialism of language, i.e., not plain vernacularism but a language elevated to lyrical height;

4. the essentialism of *décor*, i.e., not the real environment but one designed to achieve a high artistic level.

These four salient features which I call the four inner features plus the four outer features aforementioned are the *sine qua non* of the traditional Chinese theatrical style, and of this style, Mei Lanfang was a great master.

(1980)

REFLECTIONS ON MY STAGE LIFE

Mei Lanfang

Following are a few selections from Mei Lanfang's writings which throw light on how the great Chinese stage artist carried on the fine traditions of Peking Opera and at the same time made bold and genuine innovations in order to bring the performing art of this classical theatre to its highest degree of perfection.

MY FIRST APPEARANCE ON THE STAGE

The first time I went on stage I was only eleven. It was the seventh day of the seventh lunar month in the year 1905 and I played the Weaving Maid in *The Cowherd and the Weaving Maid,** a colourful opera with a fancy stage setting for the double seventh festival. My teacher, Wu Lingxian, put me on a chair to mount the magpie bridge which was decorated with a good many magpies — actually lighted candles. I was very excited as I stood there singing.

---

* An opera based on the legend of the Weaving Maid in heaven and the Cowherd, a mortal, who fell in love with each other, got married and had one son and one daughter. A few years later the Heavenly Mother summoned the Weaving Maid back but the Cowherd, taking along their children, chased after her. He nearly caught up with her when the Heavenly Mother cleft the sky with her silver hairpin and made a celestial river separating the two lovers. Later, the Heavenly Mother relented and allowed them to meet once every year on the seventh day of the seventh month. On that day the two meet each other on a bridge built by hundreds of Magpies.

Three years later I was formally enrolled as a temporary member of the Xiliancheng Company.* Although I now belonged to the company I was paid little more than an apprentice, since at that time I was performing more or less to gain theatrical experience. I received a very small sum every day, but to me it was quite satisfactory. I still remember the first time I acted with the Xiliancheng and how I took home the meagre sum I had received, proffering it to my mother with both hands. Both of us were very excited. To my mother it meant her son was now able to earn money for the family. I was then only a child of fourteen. To me, it didn't matter how big the sum was. At least I was able to bring something home to her. This was a comforting thought for a child. But to my great sorrow she fell ill the following year. She died in our humble little house on the 18th of the seventh month leaving me an orphan all on my own.

At that time I performed a daily matinée, mostly playing *qing yi* (respectable woman) roles. Sometimes I played the lead, other times I was only one of the cast. In those days, the distinction between the *qing yi* and the *hua dan* (vivacious young woman) was very clear-cut.

A person taking the *hua dan* role must give much attention to facial expression, movement and impromptu humorous dialogue. Her costume also tends towards the bold, colourful and splendid. In the Chinese classical theatre, the *hua dan* represents the lively, romantic woman. Her walk and gestures on stage differ distinctly from that of the *qing yi*, but for her the need for a good voice and a high degree of perfection in singing are not too strict. The teachers of apprentices for the theatre usually take constant and careful note of the natural talents of the pupils and assign them to different roles accord-

---

* A famous Peking Opera company formed in 1903. In the decades since it was established it had produced a number of good actors. Well-known Peking Opera artists like Ma Lianliang and Tan Fuying were both students in the company and other artists like Mei Lanfang and Zhou Xinfang were its members at one time or another.

ingly. For instance, a pupil whose facial expression is stiff, who is clumsy and heavy in build and whose eyes lack a lively look, will never be chosen to learn the *hua dan* role.

The main emphasis for the *qing yi* is on singing; the rest, such as expression and movements are of little consequence. *Qing yi* players usually need only look cold and remote as the ice and frost. When they come on stage they always adopt a sedate walk, with one hand on the stomach and the other hanging by one side. In their sedate and steady walk no swaying is allowed. In the classical theatre, the *qing yi* represents the serious obedient character, the typically respectable female. Women in the old society were usually under fairly heavy pressure. They had to carry themselves "without looking either left or right and never smile so boldly as to show the teeth". They were required to behave in a way befitting a woman who "obeys her father before her marriage, her husband after marriage, and her son when her husband is dead". When such a character appears on stage the audience asks only that she sings well. No one notices her facial expressions and gestures.

I followed the path of the family theatrical tradition established by my grandfather Mei Qiaoling. He started with *kun qu* opera and then went on to learn the *qing yi* and *hua dan* roles in Peking Opera. In his times he was considered to be very versatile to have learned so many different kinds of roles. I started by learning the *qing yi*, then I gradually tried the various other female roles (the vivacious woman, the *ingénue* and the serving maid) in *kun qu*. Later I studied the warrior maid and the lively maid in Peking Opera. I acted in modern-costume operas as well as period plays. In other words after my *début* on the stage I learned several kinds of female roles. Grandfather and I differed only in that I never attempted the comedies of the romantic maid while he never tried the acrobatic feats of the warrior maid. The reason is simple enough. He was too heavily built for acrobatics, while I felt that my temperament was not suited for the role of a witty woman who can jest and poke fun.

(*1951*)

HOW I PLAY IN MY TWO FAVOURITE OPERAS

The Drunken Beauty and *Beauty Defies Tyranny* are both my favourite operas. The former is a difficult piece which combines intricate singing and dancing. There are various dance movements like leaning backwards holding the wine cup in the teeth and sliding slowly to the ground. This can only be done properly after much training of the waist and the leg muscles. The part is therefore usually played by actors skilled in the performance of women warriors.

The story of *The Drunken Beauty* is quite simple. Emperor Ming Huang of the Tang dynasty promises to come to a feast at Hundred Flowers Pavilion with his favourite concubine Lady Yang (Yang Yuhuan). But he breaks his word and goes instead to Lady Mei in the Western Palace. Lady Yang has to feast alone. Because she is unhappy, she drinks heavily and talks and behaves in an intoxicated manner. Finally, bitter and sad, she is helped by her maids to return to her palace late at night.

In this opera, she drinks three times, and her feelings are different each time. The artist must demonstrate these three different stages. First, learning that the emperor has gone to the Western Palace, she feels lonely and disappointed. But she is afraid that the attendants will laugh at her, so she pretends not to care and keeps a dignified appearance. Then after drinking a bit, she thinks about the emperor and his other favourite, and is jealous. Raising her cup she reveals her annoyance somewhat. Finally she has had too much to drink and can no longer control herself. She smiles and imbibes recklessly until she becomes completely drunk. One can see from the title of this piece that it mainly depicts a lady in her cups. However it should be performed with discretion and not be over-exaggerated. The artist must keep in mind that here is a noble lady of the court getting drunk and forgetting herself in her loneliness and grief, not a woman of loose conduct behaving wildly after drinking. Only by interpreting it this way can one convey the spirit and produce a beautiful drama.

In 1935 during my visit to the Soviet Union a critic commented on my performance of *The Drunken Beauty* saying that I
was depicting a noble lady getting drunk and there were three
stages in my gestures and expressions. First the lady decorous-
ly screens her face with her sleeve as she drinks, next she drinks
openly, and lastly she drinks with abandon. This I think is a
very penetrating observation. Another foreign critic said to
me: "Actually when a person gets drunk, she becomes disorder-
ly and sick, a disgusting, unseemly sight. But on the stage one
mustn't show it that way, but should emphasize graceful movements and the harmony of singing and dancing so that the
audience gets a feeling of beauty." This is exactly so. We always say that on the stage one must convey a feeling of beauty;
his words show that he had the same idea.

I use *The Drunken Beauty* only as an example. An artist
should study well the character and social position of every
character he plays, and analyse with care so that he may express the emotions correctly. He should also study the good
points of other artists, grasping the main things and absorbing
the best. One must not mechanically imitate good intonations
or gestures while forgetting to adapt them in a flexible manner.

Of all the operas I have performed in, *Beauty Defies
Tyranny** is one on which I have spent the most effort. The
emotions of the daughter in this opera are very hard to describe.
There are two kinds of feelings which have to be portrayed on
stage. One is the character's joy, anger or sorrow. When
things go well, you are happy; when there is misfortune, you
show sadness. This is fairly simple. The other type is conflicting, hidden emotions. This is more difficult.

As soon as the daughter appears on the scene, she recites
these lines: "The nightingale weeps on the bough, shedding

---

* This opera tells the story of an evil minister Zhao Gao, who framed
up against Kuang Hong, an upright minister and father-in-law of his daughter, caused Kuang to be killed by the Qin emperor and was eager to present his daughter to the emperor. The daughter, however, did not yield to
pressure, but helped by a dumb maid, feigned madness and saved herself.
For details, see Appendix.

sad tears in secret." These words show that she is suffering agonies in her heart. A sudden calamity has struck. Her home has been broken and her husband has disappeared. Returning to her parents' home, she has discovered that the fabricator of the plot against her husband is her own father. Under these complex circumstances, the artist should convey her internal conflict — intense suffering and the necessity to remain calm.

She now realizes how completely heartless her father is. He wants to give her away as a gift. And the emperor is all mighty — she can never escape his clutches if he becomes interested in her. How can a weak woman like her defy him? She has therefore to devise some clever means to extricate herself. Here I try to convey her effort to keep cool.

At this critical moment, she suddenly notices her maid-servant, a mute, indicating by gestures that she should feign madness. Then I show how she forces herself to accept this plan, as a last desperate measure.

Why is it most important to depict these feelings? We are feigning already when we act a part, and the character in this opera is, in addition, feigning madness. We have to remember all the time that she is only pretending to be mad. She is not really insane, and this can only be shown through her expressions. Since the one who suggests this plan to her happens to be a dumb servant who has lost the power of speech, the daughter can only communicate with her by means of gestures and facial expressions. So from the time she considers feigning madness, one has to show three kinds of feelings: genuine feeling when she accepts the dumb maid-servant's plan, pretended feeling and feigned madness towards her father Zhao Gao, and conflicting feeling when she is pondering in doubt. All these different emotions have to be portrayed within a very short time. The performing artist has to work all this out himself. The first thing to do is to forget that you are acting and make yourself one with the part. Only then can you depict those feelings profoundly and meticulously.

Like all other arts, the Chinese classical opera has its own aesthetic basis. The Chinese classical opera is based on singing and dance movements which must follow the cadence of the music to form a certain pattern. The beautiful dance movements created by past artists are all based on gestures in real life, synthesized and accentuated to become art. And so the performing artist has this two-fold task: apart from acting his role according to the development of the story, he must also remember that his job is to express himself through beautiful dance movements. If he fails to do this, he cannot produce good art. Whether the character in the play is truly mad or is just feigning madness, the artist must see to it that all the movements on the stage are beautiful. In this opera the daughter is supposed to pull a few whiskers from Zhao Gao's beard with her middle finger and thumb, grimacing at the same time. This gives comic relief if done lightly. But it is not the least amusing if over-emphasized. Whenever I perform this part, I always see to it that the audience laughs.

The daughter feigns madness both at home and in the imperial court, but her gestures are quite different. In the imperial court her gestures should be more effusive. This is to show her fearless spirit, that she holds them all in contempt, even the emperor and his officials. It also suggests to the audience that the imperial court is a big place, quite different from her own house. When she comes out, she first sings four lines: "With lowered head I descend from the phoenix carriage. . . . I shall see what the tyrant has to say." At this moment she should look calm and ready to cope with the tense situation awaiting her.

When she goes up the steps, before paying homage to the emperor, she should pretend to dust her cap and gown like a man in a dashing and swaggering manner. This arouses the audience's interest.

When the emperor is berated by her, he grows angry, and orders his officers to cross their swords before her, to threaten her with their arms. According to tradition, this is done by two soldiers. But I felt they were not enough, so I made a change. I let four soldiers come up on all sides and besiege me with their swords. Then I shake my sleeves at them and drive them back. In this way I felt the tension was further heightened. It showed the daughter's unbending courage more strongly and intensified the drama of the episode.

After she leaves the imperial court and sees her dumb maid again, she registers sadness and joy, as if she cannot express her feelings fully. Even then I must not relax for one moment. Though the play is nearly over and I am tired, I laugh three times, with a touch of sadness, and the drama concludes in a solemn and melancholy mood.

A friend who has seen me playing the leading role in these two operas several times commented that I like to keep changing my gestures and movements. Actually I do not do so purposely. As I perform a part, new understanding of it makes me alter my gestures unconsciously. Of course you cannot change the main elements in a drama. But you can always improve your technical skill by dint of hard study. Maturity is attained slowly. You come to understand a part only after much practice. Unless you really understand a character, even if you are taught how to act it, you cannot interpret it correctly. The technical skill of a performing artist improves with the years; it cannot be forced. I admit that I have improved my art by constantly revising my technique.

There is no limit to the perfection of an art. There is a well-known saying among professionals: "The teacher gives you initial knowledge, but how far you go depends on yourself." This means that to achieve something in art, you must struggle hard and persevere. If you rely on your own talent and do not work hard, or become conceited as soon as you achieve some slight success and do not welcome criticism from all sides, it is certain you will never achieve much.

I have never felt satisfied with my performing technique. Take the opera *Beauty Defies Tyranny* for instance. I have studied this part for dozens of years, and people seem to think that this is one piece I do fairly well. But even now I keep discovering shortcomings. I remember, one day a few years ago when I was playing the part in Shanghai, it happened that my voice was not too good that day, so my acting was also somewhat different. The following day a friend made this criticism: "I like this opera of his best of all and I have seen it many times. I am full of admiration for his wonderful acting. However, in the performance yesterday, I think, he overacted a bit, and lost some of his usual balance and poise. I hope he will pay attention to this, for over-exaggeration means bad art." I took these words very seriously. Because my voice was not good that day, in order to hide my weakness in the part, I unconsciously overdid my gestures. I am very grateful that this friend pointed out my mistake, for I have always believed in balance and poise in stage art, and in not accentuating certain characteristics. This was what I have aimed at all these years. When I trespassed on my own rule, it was lucky that it was pointed out to me in good time, so that I could correct myself. It has been most helpful to me in subsequent performances.

(1951)

MY NEW OPERA *MU GUIYING TAKES COMMAND*

Some people cannot understand why I work so hard on the stage when I am already quite old. Do I have to work for my living or is it because I want to satisfy my private passion for acting? No, neither of these is the answer. The main reason is that the audience has not lost their interest in me; they are still urging me to advance, to do something new and better. They want me to bring out before a wide audience all the best I have learned in the past decades from the old masters so that the younger generation of artists can make use of it. I cannot fail them in their hope. Today many of the artistic achievements and technical improvements of past artists are gradually being forgotten, while the new generation of artists has not yet reached maturity. At this juncture, as a stage artist of the older generation I should work to the best of my ability and as much as I can. So in 1959 I produced a new opera — *Mu Guiying Takes Command*.

3

9

Early in the eleventh century there was a famous general at the northern frontier named Yang Jiye who performed many deeds of valour in the defence of the Song empire. His name is well remembered by the people and there are many heroic tales about the Yang family generals in folk legends. According to legend, Mu Guiying was the wife of Yang Jiye's grandson. When she was young, she also won many victories for the Song empire. During the wars against enemy aggression, Yang Jiye and most of his sons perished, but still the family was not trusted by the emperor. Later, Mu Guiying and her husband, together with her grandmother-in-law, retired to their home district. This story *Mu Guiying Takes Command* occurred more than twenty years after her retirement. At that time the Khitans again invaded the Song empire and a state of emergency was declared at the northern frontier. The Song emperor ordered that a tournament be held on the parade ground. The man who was victorious would be chosen as commander of the army. Mu Guiying's son Yang Wenguang and her daughter Yang Jinhua took part in the tournament. The son killed Wang Lun, the son of an evil minister Wang Qiang, and won the commander's seal. But since the son and his sister were too young, the emperor ordered that Mu Guiying, their mother, assume command. When they took the seal home, Mu Guiying, remembering past grievances, was at first unwilling to accept. After being persuaded by her grandmother-in-law, she decided to forget personal grievances and assume command at the front in order to defend the country.

To me the role of Mu Guiying is not a new one. As early as forty years ago I acted in the opera *Mu's Village Fortress* which describes how Mu Guiying meets her husband in her youth. In that opera she is shown as being intelligent, naive, brave and patriotic and the role is played by a *dao ma dan* (woman warrior) actor.

Since I knew the character of Mu Guiying, the woman general, it might have been thought that I should find little difficulty in the new opera *Mu Guiying Takes Command*.

But this was not the case. In the past I played the *dao ma dan* role and portrayed her as a young woman. In this new opera, however, Mu Guiying is a married woman who has lived through many sad experiences and is in retirement, when she becomes the commander of an army. She has to change from a passive role to an active one. Before assuming command, since she is growing old and feels depressed, she should be a *qing yi*. It has been a new departure for me to depict two different types within the same role.

The scene "Accepting the Command" is the climax of the drama. Here I have to show that Mu Guiying is unwilling because the Song emperor treated her family badly. Then I have to depict how she decides to assume command after all because she is a patriot. Such a *dénouement* is quite correct. But I felt the change was too sudden from her initial unwillingness to her acceptance and immediate exultation at the sound of drums. There seemed an emotional immaturity, something lacking in dramatic effect in this abrupt transition. It struck me that when such a great responsibility falls on one who, after all, has not fought for more than twenty years, there must be a certain mental conflict; some additions were necessary here. So I decided to make bold use of traditional form of musical accompaniment: an intermixture of loud and muted gonging, during which the heroine does not sing but simply shows by dance movements that she is reflecting deeply.

This type of accompaniment is generally used in scenes just before a battle when generals are thinking out their plan of campaign; the louder and lower sounds suggest their mental conflict. This device has seldom been used apart from battle scenes, and certainly never for a *qing yi*.

When the miming begins, I spread my sleeves and march from one side to another with a bold stride rarely used by the *qing yi*. I make fighting gestures, then go through the motion of looking at the mirror, suggesting that Mu Guiying is old and a warrior no more. I then walk back, pointing at both sides to indicate that the troops have diminished and the heroine has no able officers left. Stirring music at this point symbolizes the heroine's patriotism, but still she cannot make up her mind. Of course, there is no solution to either of the two reasons for the hesitation. At last I give an exclamation and sing the line: "Have I no love for my country and my people that I will not fight for them?" Mu Guiying is urging herself to cease hesitating, and go out like a loyal soldier and fight the enemy. I add this deliberation to give the audience a sense of the coming battle and help to build up to the climax.

Then, hands behind me, I turn my back on the audience. But when drums sound, I first retrace two steps, march to the front of the stage and spread my sleeves. Wheeling around I show a feeling of assurance, as if Mu Guiying has recaptured her youth, when she was invincible in battle. Then I walk towards the wings, turn round and again stand still with my back to the audience. At this moment to heighten the atmosphere there is the sound of horses whinnying. Then I hold the commander's seal and sing: "Who else can assume command if I refuse? Who can lead the troops if not I?" as I make a heroic exit.

Some of those who watched my performance commented that my pose when holding the commander's seal produced a strong sculptural effect. I attribute this partly to the fact that I have always taken an interest in the fine arts. A few years ago when I performed in Luoyang, I visited the famous Longmen Grottoes where many Buddhist images are cut into the hillside rock. Especially noteworthy are the great Buddhas at Feng Xian Monastery, one of which measures more than a hundred feet in height. Each of its ears alone is larger than a man. These exquisitely carved yet dignified sculptures are a rare sight. Last year when I performed in Taiyuan, I visited the famous Jin Temple and saw the images of women attendants beside the Holy Mother made by Song dynasty artists. All these figures are holding something, some smiling, some frowning. They combine beauty with realism, yet no two are alike. I lingered there enchanted for a long time, unable to tear myself away. Such art, constantly seen and remembered, helps an actor greatly by enriching his experience. Hence my bearing when holding the seal in this opera was based un-consciously on those past impressions, though if you ask me which particular image I was imitating, I would not be able to answer you, for I did not deliberately imitate any single gesture. We know that all forms of art should absorb nourishment from various sources, but we must bear in mind the principle of taking over the spirit and not merely copying the form. If we borrow in a mechanical or dogmatic manner, we cannot create true art.

My experience has been that when you first learn to act you have few expressions and gestures at your finger tips. Gradually you acquire more and more. But when you are really experienced you synthesize them down into a few which are the most suitable. Only then can you become really skilful in your performances.

(1959)

ARTISTIC PERCEPTION AND JUDGEMENT

A person usually tends a bit towards hero-worship when watching the performance of a famous artist. It is easy to hold his attention, and therefore easy to move him; the per-formance does not just drift over his head. On the other hand, it is more difficult to recognize the merits of an artist who has not made his name although possessing a good technique. When viewing a stage performance you should not ignore the lesser known artists, for this is the opportunity to practise your artistic perception and judgement.

When I was young, each time I finished playing my part, I would watch the show from the wings. Sometimes I saw some minor parts being played by actors who did not have a good appearance or a good voice, and the audience paid them little attention. But backstage they were treated with great respect. I realized that these were veteran artists who had good technique, but frankly speaking, at first I could not see why they were considered good. Only after watching and

listening carefully over a long period did I come to understand
that such artists knew a great deal, were very meticulous in
their art and really surpassed the others in many ways.

For instance, when actors A, B and C play secondary roles
in an opera you may not see what outstanding talents they
have.   But if one day the actor B should die, and someone
else takes his place, you realize immediately that B has certain
talents which his substitute does not possess.   Through such
actual experience you learn to improve your artistic perception.

Apart from learning from actors playing your kind of roles,
you also should study the art of actors playing other roles in
order to broaden your outlook. Watching a new type of
Chinese drama or a foreign drama is also a good way to train
your artistic perception.   It is difficult to appreciate the good
things in a drama which is entirely new to you, but if you
study it patiently, you can gradually recognize its good points
and shortcomings.   You should tell the experts in that form
of drama what you think are good or bad whenever there is
an opportunity, so that you may learn their reactions to your
amateurish views.   When you can criticize correctly a new
form of art, it means that you have improved your artistic
perception and judgement.

You should do this patiently and consistently, not just
when the mood suits you.   Otherwise, you lose opportunities
to improve your art.   Let me mention one example: I remember once I went to a local opera I had never seen before.   My first impression was that the singing and dialogue
were ridiculous and the music jarring.   I wanted to get up
and walk out.   Then I reminded myself to be patient and not
forget my profession and purpose in seeing this drama.   I
forced myself to study it.   Suddenly I found I could understand
some of its good points.   My eyes and my ears became more
receptive.   After studying such operas several times, I not
only could understand them, but learned to enjoy the performance of some of the actors.   In the dozens of years of my
stage career, I have always tried to learn new things although
sometimes I lost patience and became subjective.   If I had not

reminded myself in time, I would have lost some good opportunities. It is entirely up to yourself whether or not you improve your perception and judgement.

This is so not only when studying performances on stage; it is even more applicable when studying with a teacher. The teacher gives us our basic training. In the beginning, naturally we have no artistic perception or judgement; we can only imitate his every sound, every gesture. After we reach a certain level, we have to concentrate on the teacher's special technique. For example, at the time I studied the *kun qu* opera *The Peony Pavilion* under veteran *kun qu* artist Jiao Huilan, Jiao had already long since given up the stage. My impression of him was that of a wizened old man. But when he started demonstrating gestures, I felt that the aged man wearing an old fur coat had ceased to exist. I could only see the exquisite movements of the heroine in the play. I thought then, if someone ignorant of the art was watching, he would think it was extremely funny.

Another veteran artist Chen Delin also taught me the same role, and he also gave me the same impression. Their performances without make-up were just as enthralling as their performances on stage. This is real art. When you are with such veteran artists, apart from learning the many fine movements they teach, there is also a great deal they cannot put into words which you discover just by watching closely.

When you develop perception, not only can you emulate your teachers — you discover things worth noticing everywhere. For instance, you observe the expressions of a man sitting leisurely, those of a person who has lost his child on the road, the way a good calligraphist holds his pen, the adept movements of a woman washing clothes, and so on. All unusual expressions or highly rhythmic movements can be grasped by a person with a sharp sense of perception, then translated into art and adapted for the stage.

When an actor tries to depict a certain character in a drama, apart from learning from past literature and the accumulated experience of famous artists of the past, he has to absorb new material from life to enrich that character and give new life to traditional art. If he is unable to differentiate the good from the bad, the beautiful from the ugly, the things he absorbs from life will be unsuitable, or even bad.

Sometimes the artist intends to absorb useful material from life, but because he cannot differentiate the good from the bad, the beautiful from the ugly, and has not studied properly the experience of past artists, or having studied cannot grasp this experience thoroughly and treat it seriously enough, then he does not know what things can be adapted to the stage and what cannot.

Take for instance the character of the Monkey King. When played by a good actor, the audience feels that he is a hero, a god; on stage he looks splendid. His make-up and movements convey his heroic spirit, while at the same time he displays the characteristic agility of the monkey. That is how the character should be depicted. However, some actors playing this role do not convey the same feeling. They try hard to imitate a real monkey, bringing to the stage a lot of unbecoming gestures. Such an indiscriminate adherence to nature is a very bad tendency.

Of course, an artist should be inventive in his stage art, but this originality must come through study. If he has not studied widely, if he has not properly digested past experiences, he will not be able to find the right means of expression. He will only be able to invent things out of his head. This not only hampers the development of his art, it may even lead him astray.

(1956)

MEI LANFANG AS SEEN BY HIS FOREIGN AUDIENCES AND CRITICS

Mei Shaowu

"When Mei Lanfang was playing a death scene a spectator sitting next to me exclaimed with astonishment at one of his gestures. One or two people sitting in front of us turned round indignantly and sshhh'd. They behaved as if they were present at the real death of a real girl." This was how the outstanding German playwright Bertolt Brecht wrote about the stage effect of Peking Opera after he saw my father's performance in Moscow in 1935. Brecht always admired Peking Opera as a performing art and actually applied some of its techniques to his own plays.

EARLY EFFORTS TO POPULARIZE PEKING OPERA AMONG FOREIGN AUDIENCES

My father's artistic skill on stage fascinated many foreign playwrights and audiences, notwithstanding the cultural barrier between the East and West. From the time he received Peking Opera training, when he was eight, to his stage *début* when he was only 11, up to the time of his death in 1961 at the age of 67 (except for the eight years in the period of the War of Resistance Against Japan during which he grew a moustache to show his determination not to give performances in Japanese-occupied

Mei Shaowu, the second son of Mei Lanfang, is a translator of Western literature and a staff member of the National Beijing Library.

Shanghai), he had performed Peking Opera on the stage for as long as half a century. While enjoying great popularity at home, he also went abroad several times between 1919 and 1956 to introduce the art of Peking Opera to the people of Japan, the United States and the Soviet Union. During his successful performance tours in these countries, which earned him international fame, he established ties of friendship with people overseas, many being luminaries in the world of art and literature.

FIRST PERFORMANCE BEFORE A FOREIGN AUDIENCE

According to the earliest record available, he gave his first performance before a foreign audience in 1916. It was in the fall of that year when the committee of a teachers' club (its members were Americans teaching in schools they had founded in north China) hit upon the idea of watching some Peking Opera at a social evening for a change. So, Father was invited to stage his new opera *Lady Chang E Flies to the Moon** in the banquet hall of the then Chinese Foreign Ministry compound. More than 300 Americans attended and were intrigued by the fine performance given by that young actor who had made the best of the artistry of classical Chinese theatre. After that, a Peking Opera with Father playing the leading role became one of the two "musts" for foreign guests visiting China, the other being the world famous Great Wall.

VISITS TO JAPAN

In 1919 Father paid his first visit to Japan, staging Peking Opera for the first time in a foreign land. His operatic troupe appeared in Tokyo, Osaka, Nagasaki and other cities. Its performances were warmly acclaimed by the Japanese public, with an especially strong response from those of cultural circles, such as the sinologists Trajiro Naito and Dr. Naoki Kano and the

---

* This opera tells the story of Lady Chang E, who unwittingly drinks the elixir of immortality, flies to the moon and is chosen by the moon fairies as their Queen because of her surpassing beauty.

dramatist Seiji Aoki. They all wrote articles discussing the origin and evolution of the classical Chinese theatre and praising Father's artistic accomplishments. Many Japanese actors vied with each other in imitating his dance movements which they called "the Mei dance". The Japanese *kabuki* actor Utauemon Nakamura, for one, later staged Mei's *The Maiden in Heaven Showering Flowers* in Japanese in Asakusa.

In 1924 Father visited Japan for the second time and it turned out to be a still greater success than the first one and his name became more widely known. In August, 1926, the Japanese *kabuki* company headed by Jinya Morota and Kakiko Murata came to China to give performances. Father received them and appeared on stage with the Japanese artists, which created quite a sensation in Beijing (Peking).

Three decades later, after the founding of New China, Father made his third and most meaningful visit to Japan. It was in the summer of 1956, when he led a Chinese Peking Opera delegation to perform in Tokyo and other cities. This marked a major event in the cultural exchange between the two countries. At that time, diplomatic relations between China and Japan had still to be restored. Father went there on a mission entrusted to him by the late Premier Zhou Enlai to forge new friendly ties between the two countries. During the visit, he met many old friends in Japanese theatrical circles, talked shops with the famous *kabuki* actors Ennosuke Ichikawa, Ganuemon Nakamura and Chojuro Kawahasaki and had extensive discussions with other Japanese artists and scholars. Prince Mikasa once attended his performance. At the end of the show, the Prince went backstage and extended his congratulations to Father, saying: "Both your acting and the costumes are most beautiful. Yours is an art both classic and imbued with the vitality of youth. I admire it." "My brother (the Mikado)," he added, "also watched you on TV in the palace. He too admires the superb skills of the Chinese Peking Opera delegation headed by you."

ENTERTAINING FOREIGN GUESTS AT HOME,
PROPOSAL FOR U.S. TOUR

The year 1926 saw Father very active in receiving and entertaining his foreign admirers.

When the Swedish Crown Prince, who was later to become King Gustav VI Adolf and his consort visited China that year, they wished to see a Peking Opera performed by Mei Lanfang. So Father gave a tea party at home and put on a performance to entertain the royal couple. He also gave the Prince an antique stone seal as a souvenir. In 1956 when my younger sister Mei Baoyue visited Stockholm as a member of the Chinese Traditional Song and Dance Ensemble, she was received by King Gustav VI Adolf who recalled and described to her his meeting with Father 30 years ago. The Swedish sovereign also mentioned the stone seal, which, he said, had been given away to the Royal Museum for the public to see together with the other artifacts in his collection.

As early as in 1925, a group of American tourists, upon their return to the United States from China, told their folks at home a great deal about Father's performances. So in 1926, the U.S. Minister to China at that time, John Van A. MacMurray, proposed that Father should go and perform in the United States. He said he was ready to do his best to push forward this project, which, he thought, would help the American people understand Chinese theatrical art better and promote friendship between the two peoples. On the fifth day of the fifth moon, a traditional Chinese festival, Father invited MacMurray and members of the American Legation to see his new mythological opera *The Red Snake and the Golden Pin* in appreciation of the proposal. This proposal was later reaffirmed by another U.S. envoy, this time the outgoing U.S. Minister Dr. Paul Reinsch. But the project was not realized until the end of 1929 when Father and his troupe left China for a six-month U.S. tour.

Other guests from abroad who met Father in those years included the Italian soprano Galli-Curci, the British writer Somerset Maugham and the American dancers Ruth St. Denis and Ted Shawn.

In appreciation of my father's activities in the promotion of friendship with people from abroad, Julean Arnold, then the American Commercial Attaché in Beijing, wrote on November 29, 1926:

> To those who have been identified with the life in Peking during the past 10 or 12 years, it has been satisfying to note the manner in which Mei Lanfang has availed himself of the opportunities he has enjoyed of popularizing the Chinese drama among foreign audiences. This aside from the pleasure which he may have accorded his own people in his plays on the Chinese stage, he may be proud of what he has done to educate the foreign public in China to a better appreciation of Chinese drama and Chinese acting. . . . Thus we are interested in Mei Lanfang, firstly because of his superb histrionic talents, secondly because of his excellent work in elevating the Chinese drama and Chinese actors to a higher plane in society, and thirdly because he is a student possessed with initiative and a desire to improve the Chinese stage so that it may more truly depict the art and culture of the Chinese people. We wish him every success, for whatever he does towards aiding Westerners in a better appreciation of Chinese art and culture, contributes towards a better mutual understanding between the East and the West.

SUCCESSFUL U.S. TOUR

The time: February 26, 1930. The place: The 49th Avenue Theatre, Broadway, New York. The occasion: The gala première of Peking Opera in the United States. Despite the Great Depression, Peking Opera proved to be such a big attraction to the American people that all the tickets for the following two weeks were sold out in three days.

My father was then 36. For many years he had cherished the desire to introduce the art of Peking Opera to the American

Mei Lanfang as Lady Chang E in *Lady Chang E Flies to the Moon* (1915). This opera is the story of Lady Chang E, who unwittingly drinks the elixir of immortality, flies to the moon and is chosen by the moon fairies as their Queen because of her surpassing beauty.

Mei Lanfang's visit to Japan in 1924.

Mei Lanfang's visit to Japan in 1956.

Mei Lanfang's arrival in San Francisco during his U.S. tour in 1930. Mayor James Rolph Jr. escorted him from railway station to the Capitol Theatre where a welcome meeting was held.

A performance given by Mei Lanfan... Street Theatre, Broadway, New Yo...

M...
sta...

he 49th
n 1930.

Mei Lanfang and Charlie Chaplin.

fang in *Rainbow Pass*
during his U.S. tour.

Mei Lanfang and Mary Pickford.

Mei Lanfang poses with the president of Pomona College after receiving an honorary doctorate from the college.

Mei Lanfang and Konstantin Stanislavsky.

Mei Lanfang with Erwin Piscator (centre) and Eisenstein.

Mei Lanfang and Paul Robeson (1935).

people and at the same time study foreign theatrical art. The 24-member Mei Troupe headed by him left for the States in the winter of 1929. In the next six months it visited many cities, including Seattle, New York, Chicago, Washington, D.C., San Francisco, Los Angeles, San Diego and Honolulu. There, in the United States, he staged *The Fisherman's Revenge, By the Fen River Bend, The Drunken Beauty, The King's Parting with His Favourite, Killing the "Tiger", Chun Xiang Upsets the Study, The Maiden in Heaven Showering Flowers* and *Rainbow Pass.* He also performed the sleeve dance in *Lady Shangyuan,* the feather dance in *Beauty Xi Shi,* the sickle dance in *Lady Chang E Flies to the Moon,* the cup and tray dance in *Ma Ku Wishing Wang Mu a Long Life* and the sword dance in *Hongxian Stealing the Box.*

AMERICAN HOSPITALITY

In every city the Mei Troupe visited, a group of patrons with the mayor at its head was there to serve as a sort of reception committee. In San Francisco tens of thousands of people went to the railroad station to greet the troupe on arrival. Mayor James Rolph Jr. made a welcome speech in the square outside the station amidst thunderous applause. Accompanied by the Mayor, Father was driven to San Francisco's Capitol Theatre to attend a get-together, "Welcome to the Great Artist Mei Lanfang". He was also invited to give a special performance in Washington, D.C., for people in political circles, and was later presented with a set of 24 presidential medals as a keepsake.

Father was even more warmly received by people of literary and art circles. He came to know many of them, such as dramatists David Belasco and Stark Young, film stars Charles Chaplin, Douglas Fairbanks, Mary Pickford and the famous director Cecil B. de Mille. As the guest of the Fairbanks, he stayed in their villa "Fairford" for a few days and visited various film studios in Hollywood. Later, when Fairbanks and Chaplin came to China, Father reciprocated their generous

hospitality with gusto. While he was in the States, many painters and sculptors asked him for sittings, and he and the other
members of the troupe were admitted as honorary members
of New York's Theatrical Society.

People of the academic world also showed great interest in
his performances which were attended by many university pres-
idents and professors, who were of the opinion that Peking
Opera as a theatrical form was of great literary and artistic
value. Receptions or forums were held in Columbia University,
Chicago University, San Francisco University and Hawaii
University, where Father introduced the art of Peking Opera
to the audiences. University of Southern California and
Pomona College both conferred on him honorary doctorates (of
literature) in recognition of his highly accomplished theatrical
skill and the effort he put into introducing an art of the Orient
to the West, in promoting friendly feelings between the peoples
of China and the United States and the promotion of world
cultural exchanges in general.

SENTIMENTS OF THE AUDIENCES

Warmer still were the sentiments of the audiences. At the
end of every performance there were at least 15 curtain calls.
At the end of the last performance in New York, the audience
was reluctant to leave the theatre, wishing to shake hands with
Father, who readily agreed. So they formed a long queue walking up to the stage to shake hands with him in turn. This lasted
for a long time and there seemed to be no end to the queue
as it turned out many of them re-joined it for the second time,
in order to have another handshake with Mei Lanfang!

The American public became keenly interested in Peking
Opera. One store in New York borrowed some of the magnificent Peking Opera costumes for display in a shop window,
while at a flower show a new species was named "Mei Lanfang"! In Honolulu, the natives at a reception wrote a song
in their own language entitled *Wishing Mei Lanfang Success;*
later, when my father embarked on board ship for home, the

crowd sang another song they wrote — *The Song of Mei Lan-fang* — to bid him farewell at the quay-side.

MEI LANFANG IN THE EYES OF U.S. CRITICS

Many literary and art critics in their reviews showed their admiration for the art of Peking Opera and Father's artistic excellence.   Stark Young wrote in *The New Republic* (March 5, 1930):

> His make-up, that overlay of carmines and darker tones, is the most beautiful I have ever seen in a theater. . . .   The famous hands are curiously like those in Boticelli, Simone Martini and other painters of the 15th century . . . incredible, trained in the conventions and dance of the Chinese actor's art.

And John Martin wrote in *The New York Times* on February 23, 1930: "His voice, for all its falsetto strangeness, is of exceptional beauty."

In *The New York Evening Post* (February 17, 1930), an article by John Mason Brown observed: "Mei Lanfang possesses amazingly expressive eyes and a mobile face that registers with the utmost sensitivity each passing emotion."

"HIGHEST POINT IN THE SEASON'S THEATRE"

The fact that Peking Opera is an art with a fine time-honoured tradition impressed itself upon a number of American theatrical critics.   Stark Young also remarked:

> In an art that belongs within the tradition of an old race, and in the presence of an artist considered by them a great artist, a good part of our attendance must be taken with humility. . . .   In this performance of Mei Lanfang I saw enough to see that for me it was the highest point in the season's theater and in any season since Duse's visit and the Moscow Art Theater's production of Chekhov's plays.

Justin Brooks Atkinson, the well-known dramatic critic who is now in his late eighties, also wrote in praise of him:

... for the drama of Peking, whence Mr. Mei and his actors come, has almost no point of similarity to the drama with which we are familiar; and the barrier of language is nothing by comparison with the barrier of a completely exotic art. It is styled, conventionalized and as old as the hills. But it is as beautiful as an old Chinese vase or tapestry. If you can purge yourself of the sophomoric illusion that it is funny, merely because it is different, you can begin to appreciate something of exquisite loveliness in pantomime and costume, and you may feel yourself vaguely in contact, not with the sensation of the moment, but with the strange ripeness of centuries. Perhaps you may even have a few bitter moments of reflecting that although our own theatrical form is enormously vivid it is rigid, and never lives so freely in terms of imagination as this one does. (*The New York Times*, February 17, 1930.)

"GREEK AND ELIZABETHAN PARALLELS"

When Stark Young called on my father at a New York hotel where Father was staying, he told Father how the Peking Opera he had seen reminded him of ancient Greek theatre and that of the Elizabethan age and so it suddenly dawned on him that he had found the key to the solution of some problems in his theatrical studies. He said that he was so happy because after seeing Peking Opera he was able to understand the ancient Greek theatre even better. In his article "Mei Lanfang and His Company in Repertory" published in *New Republic*, he had already noted "the Greek and Elizabethan parallels in this Chinese theatre". Later he discussed the point further in the article entitled "Mei Lanfang" which appeared in the *Theatre Arts Monthly* (Vol. 14, April, 1930). He noted:

The qualities reminiscent of Greece represent for China a natural way of thought, a spirit deeply inherent. There are not only the patent resemblances like the men in female roles, the Chinese faces often painted into masks, with traditional styles and conventional meanings, scarcely to be distinguished from the actual masking in Attic Theatres, the limitation in setting, there are also the resemblances in qualities that proceed from the inmost characteristics of mind and spirit. There are the fixed patterns for exits and entrances and stage movement, there is the use of dancing medium, in the fullest sense of the term, the basis of musical accompaniment, musical accentuation, the rising into music where the emotion demands the very fullest expression, there is the fusion of words, speech, singing, music, dancing and *décor* into one art. There are the standard scenes, built on familiar patterns, set scenes as it were, which, as with many of our musical forms, are to be enjoyed and admired for the treatment afforded them — recognition scenes, parting scenes, scenes based on irony, dialectic scenes and so on. There is the search for pattern, and the subordination of personal emotion to some passionate abstraction and secure outline. There is the unceasing stylization throughout. There is the intention of beauty, grace or exaltation.

"DEXTEROUS REALISM"

Although Peking Opera has often been looked upon as an art without realism, conventionalized in acting, quite unreal and unnatural, Stark Young looked at it differently with an excellent view of his own. In his opinion, the acting in Peking Opera is real, not as expressed in real life, but artistically real, which the audience finds even more convincing than in the real-life version.

This Chinese theater is spoken of as completely unrealistic art, entirely ideal in character. But while this is in a larger sense true, we must be careful not to be misled. This theater art of Mei Lanfang's is not completely without realism, not in the sense that a cubistic painting would be, an abstract Arabic decoration, a geometric dance design. Its exact parallel is Chinese painting and sculpture. In these, the impression that remains in the memory is of the abstract and decorative, but we are constantly surprised at the exactitude with nature, a leaf, a bough, a bird, a hand, or a mantle, has been observed and are amazed at the dazzling notation of characteristic details and at the manner in which they are made to supercede and concentrate their own actuality. This exact notation is marvellously set into the whole work of art, which taken in its completeness, is ideal and dreamlike. To judge even by their common paintings and statuettes, the delight felt by the Chinese in this dexterous realism combined with tradition, convention and abstract pattern, must be very strong. We are to remember this when we hear it said that Mei Lanfang's art is wholly unrealistic. We must also remember that one of the things to learn from this Chinese theater art is not the need for unrealism or its contrary, but rather the exactness of the degree to which, in every part of it, realism is employed. The gestures, the narration, the acting, even the much discussed falsetto voice employed for the female roles, the movements, and so on, all are the same distance from the actual; which is another way of saying that the whole achieves a total unity of style.

Young's view was more or less shared by R.D. Skinnen who wrote in the March issue of *Commonweal* in 1930:

At least seven hundred years of unbroken tradition lie behind the conventions of classical Chinese drama. Certain gestures, certain details of costume and make-up and certain stage properties have come to represent certain well-understood realities as clearly as if they were printed labels. I understood that Mr. Mei objects to the word symbolism as describing these conventions and prefers the word pattern-ism — largely because symbolism in Western civilization has what he considers a cruder significance. He feels that Chinese theatrical conventions are the result of abstracting from a certain reality its essential pattern, whereas Western symbolism consists more in representing some object or emotion by some quite different object. It is quite sufficient to acknowledge that the Chinese drama seeks to convey the most universal elements of action and emotion, by not confusing them with particular time or place or form, and that his effort is successful even to Occidental eyes.

"ACTOR, SINGER AND DANCER COMBINED"

The ingenious combination of acting, singing and dancing in Peking Opera also drew the attention of American critics. There was Robert Littell, who wrote in *New York World* on February 17, 1930:

After he has been on the stage three minutes it is obvious that Mei Lanfang is one of the most extraordinary actors you have ever seen. An actor, singer and dancer combined, and combined so that you never see the boundary between these three arts, which as a matter of fact in the Chinese theater are indissolubly one. When you see him on the stage you find yourself in some timeless region as lovely and harmonious as an old fairy story. You forget that he is a man playing women's parts, according to immemorial custom, in a curious but irresistible falsetto voice. You forget everything but the picture he is making, as strong and delicate in every eloquent gesture as an old Chinese painting, very beautiful to look at for the costumes and poses alone, but also full of immensely subtle dignity and repose. And then think of our own surface, improvised acting, born yesterday and old stuff tomorrow.... It cannot be described, at least so soon after the first gulp of astonishment and joy. Nothing like this has ever been seen before in New York.

In his article *Mei Lanfang* which appeared in *Theatre Arts Monthly* Vol. 14, April, 1930, Stark Young wrote:

I noticed in Mei Lanfang's acting that the rhythms of the body are complete throughout. If a gesture is made with the right hand it not only proceeds from the right shoulder (in much of the acting we see hereabouts not even that occurs) but affects the left shoulder as well; so that the entire torso falls into the justly related rhythms. The head is constantly moving, subtly alive on the neck, a motion that may often be unnoticed, as we may overlook the vibration of line and plane in fine sculpture. The use of the sleeves, from which hand the long white cuffs far down below the hands, is, in Mei Lanfang, regarded by his Chinese public as the height of all his accomplishments. The variety of these usages and conventions a foreigner could only observe after a long familiarity with his art, but the beauty and drama of the dance that he creates from them is evident. . . . You see the sleeves go up, mildly fluttered, like a white dove, or even hear the flutter of wings in quick flight; a thing so subtly done and perfect that you can hardly believe it happened, and yet it was done with great certainty and design, even to its exact position on the stage.

Commenting on the sword dance in *The King's Parting with His Favourite*, noted dance critic Mary F. Watkins wrote the following in *The Dance Magazine* (May 1930): "It is a tour de force of adroitness, skill and grace, tied up in form and symbolism, but in no sense impeded by them." Another critic, William Bolitho, spoke even more highly of Father's skill in dancing on the stage:

To me, Mei Lanfang is above all a dancer; and as such I would not hesitate to put him in the very highest class. . . . In his sword dance from the "Heroic Maid" (meaning Lady Yu Ji in the opera) it is my considered opinion that he has reached one of the supreme possibilities. (*New York World*, February 20, 1930)

Ted Shawn, well-known past master of the art of dancing in the United States, said at that time: "From Mei Lanfang you will get something invaluable and incalculable and unique toward the building of your artistic experience and education."

"AMBASSADOR OF CHINESE CULTURE"

Two years after Father's visit to the United States, Stark Young wrote a long article "Ambassador in Art" for the *New Republic* in which, with a streak of nostalgic feeling, he recalled those memorable days spent watching Father's performances. Young recalled:

> Mei Lanfang had been accustomed to three performances a week, here he was obliged to give eight. He brought 45 trunks of costumes and repertory of 200 pieces ... he bore this stage strain almost to exhaustion, as he bore the endless entertainments, after his serene life in his own home in Peiping (Beijing) as a poet, musician, wrestler, dancer, art collector and student of the classics. ... I am trying to indicate the extent to which Mr. Mei and his companions regarded themselves as ambassadors of Chinese culture and the great labour to which they put themselves in that cause.

While Father was giving performances in the United States, the theatrical critic Robert Littell urged the public in an article to go and see Peking Opera. Littell wrote:

> Final week! — Mei Lanfang will give his last performance next Saturday. If you have not seen him, and do not take this last opportunity, some day you will be sorry. Some day your grandchildren, gathering round the plaid shawl over your knees, will shout down your ear trumpet, "Grandpapa, tell us about the famous Chinese actor and how he came to America and overcame the barrier of language with his delicate stylized gestures." And if you can mumble your praise of *The Drunken Beauty* and show them how the fisherman and his daughter rocked an imaginary boat, the little darlings will run away and let you go on reading "Fifty Years of the Theater Guild".

True, those who saw Father perform in the United States and who are still around, must have many grandchildren by now. In the summer of 1978 when a Chinese Performing Art Company visited the United States, I was gladdened to read an item from a newspaper about how a grey-haired old lady in her eighties recalled seeing Mei Lanfang on the American stage and spoke of the time-honoured friendship between the peoples of China and the United States. Maybe, I told myself, she is one of those who could show their grandchildren how the fisherman and his daughter rocked the imaginary boat as Littell had suggested!

A GREAT STAGE SUCCESS IN THE SOVIET UNION (1935)

At the invitation of the All-Union Society for Cultural Relations with Foreign Countries (VOKS), Father gave performances in Moscow and Leningrad in March and April, 1935. A VOKS reception committee was set up for this purpose and members of the committee included K.S. Stanislavsky, V.I. Nemirovich-Danchenko, W.E. Meyerhold, S.M. Eisenstein and other well-known figures of Soviet literary and art circles.

My father made a great stage success in the Soviet Union. Those who went to see his performances included well-known writers like Maxim Gorky and Alexi Tolstoy. Enthusiastic theatre-goers often waited outside the opera house hoping to get a glimpse of my father off stage. Children, when seeing a well-dressed Chinese on the street, invariably cried out: "Mei Lanfang!"

PRESS COMMENTS

The Soviet journalist Karl Radek wrote in *Izvestia:*

Although we know nothing about the Chinese language, nor the special features of the Chinese theater, Mei's performances have really surprised us. He has the ability to play female roles in a language strange to us and yet completely spellbind the audience with his artistic charm while presenting such lively images on the stage that one could believe them to be real.

S. Radlov, a dramatic critic, wrote:

Mei Lanfang, as the doyen of the Chinese theater, enjoys a position parallel to that of the famous Russian actress Khmmissarzhevskaya. If every detail of his acting designed to bring out a character's mental activity is carefully observed, it can be found that every movement he makes has a profound meaning. . . . The Chinese theater, as I see it, is a mixed art. . . . Our playwrights, choreographers and opera directors should try and find a way to create something new, a kind of song and dance drama combining the two arts into one. . . . Moreover, Chinese actors have received training not only in singing and dancing but also in acrobatics and martial skills and their versatility is truly amazing. In contrast, no rigid training is required of our own actors of the modern theater, and this is one of our shortcomings.

Quite a few critics spoke of Father's many-sided talents and emphasized his great contributions to the development of Chinese theatrical art, describing him as "the innovator of Chinese Peking Opera" and adding "always a bold and genuine innovator who at the same time had no wish to give up the old tradition". An article in the magazine *Workers and Theatre* was of the opinion that Father's performances in the Soviet Union should be regarded as a new milestone along the road of cultural exchange between the two countries.

SWAPPING EXPERIENCES

While in Moscow, he called on Stanislavsky, Meyerhold, Eisenstein and also Erwin Piscator, the originator of Epic Drama later developed by Bertolt Brecht, and on the British playwright Gordon Greig who was then visiting the Soviet Union. The famous Soviet ballerina Ulanova personally invited Father to watch her performance in *Swan Lake*.

He was also asked to speak on Chinese theatrical art at the Masters of Art Clubs in Moscow and Leningrad. At these talks he demonstrated on the spot the various hand gestures, stage steps and singing peculiar to Peking Opera. The attendance consisted mainly of well-known actors and actresses, who found his speech and demonstration most informative and inspiring and dubbed him "Master of Masters." Brecht, who was present, wrote later to ask: "Is there any actor in the West (with the exception of one or two comedians) who can, like Mei Lanfang, in an evening dress, perform the essentials of his stagecraft before a group of professionals in a room without any special lighting device?"

STANISLAVSKY'S INTERPRETATION

My father became a good friend of Stanislavsky's, who saw Father as a great contemporary actor and artist. One episode Father liked to recall about was Stanislavsky's interpretation of his stagecraft. There was an old lady in the Soviet Union who had several times seen a certain drama performed by Father. She had noticed that his acting was not exactly the same at each performance. She wanted to know why. Before Father explained, Stanislavsky who was present at the occasion interpolated: "Why, madame, acting by Mr. Mei is a free movement guided by the laws of the art." Father liked the explanation, which means that an actor must first of all respect the laws of his art and on that basis, he can make innovations.

Stanislavsky was then in his seventies. At the first meeting Father was immediately struck by his sincerity and modesty and his air of an accomplished artist. They met several times to discuss and exchange their theatrical experiences. In 1953 when Father was in Moscow in transit, Khmisaryevsky, a famous Soviet director, told Father how Stanislavsky mentioned Father's name and spoke of their friendship before his students and actors during a rehearsal of the last play he directed.

EISENSTEIN'S APPRAISAL

Father's performances in the Soviet Union were hailed by world-famous Soviet film director Eisenstein, who at a discussion forum gave his impression of Peking Opera as follows:

Earlier I was told that theaters in the East are all the same. I have seen Japanese dramas before and now I have seen Chinese ones. I have now come to see that a Japanese drama is as different from a Chinese one as the Roman theater was different from that of Greece, or the early American theatre from that of Europe. In a Chinese drama, the moods of joy, anger, sadness and happiness are conventionalized but not necessarily stereotyped. All the advantages of the principle of realism found in Russian drama can be found almost completely in Chinese drama....

Mr. Mei is not just a performing artist, he is also a scholar studying the possibility of further developing the characteristics of this ancient theatrical art which combines movement, music and ancient costumes into one....

To introduce the art of Peking Opera to the Soviet public, Eisenstein, with Father's consent and co-operation, directed and filmed a few scenes from *Rainbow Pass* in a Moscow studio to show all the salient features of Father's stagecraft.

Before the two parted, Eisenstein gave Father a copy of the British periodical *Close Up* (Vol. VIII, No. 3) which carried his article "The Principle of Film Form". The journal was autographed in English: "To Mr. Mei Lanfang, the greatest master of form, my essential article on the problem. S.M. Eisenstein, Moscow, 1935."

FRIENDSHIP WITH TAGORE

Among Father's many friends abroad, his unusual friendship with the great Indian poet Rabindranth Tagore must be mentioned.

Tagore visited China in May, 1924. His friends in Chinese literary and art circles staged his play *Chitra* in English to celebrate his 64th birthday. The auditorium of the Peking (Beijing) Union Medical College in the eastern part of the city was crowded with well wishers on that day, May 8. Tagore took his seat in the middle of the third row next to my father. After the performance, he told Father that while he was pleased to see his own play staged in China, he was more interested in seeing a Peking Opera performed by Father.

On the evening of May 19, Father staged *The Goddess of the River Luo* and Tagore was invited to attend. In a scarlet gown which was the formal dress of Visva-Bharati University, the Indian poet watched attentively throughout the performance and afterwards thanked Father backstage.

The next day at noon, Father and others gave a farewell dinner in Tagore's honour. While commenting on Father's performance with words of encouragement, Tagore complained that the *décor* for such a mythological drama was too plain, suggesting that hues of red, green, yellow, black and purple should be used on the stage, and the stage should be decorated with fancy rocks, flowers and other plants like a "fairyland" . . . . Father readily accepted the idea and the *décor* for this particular scene in *The Goddess of the River Luo* was finally designed anew.

Tagore wrote a poem dedicated to Father. It was written on a silk fan with a Chinese brush in the Bengali original with an English translation of his own:

> *You are veiled, my beloved,*
> *in a language I don't know,*
> *As a hill that appears like a cloud,*
> *behind its mask of mist.*

In the spring of 1961, on the occasion of the 100th anniversary of the birth of the Indian poet, Father showed the fan to many friends. Prof. Shi Zhen, with the help of Prof. Wu Xiaoling, both being well versed in Bengali and graduates from Visva Bharati University, had the poem translated into Chinese.

Tagore had wanted Father to visit India with his troupe, but Father never found an opportunity to go.

WITH BERNARD SHAW AND PAUL ROBESON

When George Bernard Shaw visited China in 1933, he specially requested a meeting with my father. When Shaw asked him why the noisy drums and gongs in the Peking Opera were necessary Father explained that this was probably because the opera was a folk art at first performed in the open air and the drums and gongs were then used to attract people to the show and this tradition had been kept to this day.

In 1935, after his visit to the Soviet Union, Father toured Europe to study the European theatre. He arrived in London in June and met Shaw again; there he also made the acquaintance of James Barrie, who gave Father a collection of his own plays. In London Father went to the theatre every night; he also attended a performance entitled *Stevedores* by the American Negro singer Paul Robeson with great interest. Back in 1930 when Father was visiting the United States he already knew Robeson by name but they had never met in person. Now, five years later, the two finally met in London and exchanged views on singing. Mrs. Paul Robeson (Eslanda Goode Robeson) presented Father with a copy of her own book *Paul Robeson, Negro* as a souvenir.

To conclude, I can see that Father did not make life-long efforts to popularize Peking Opera among foreign audiences in vain. In the last two decades, many people abroad have been studying Peking Opera and many operas have been translated into English. There are even non-Chinese actors who have themselves performed Peking Opera on the stage.

Here in our country, Peking Opera is now being revived after ten years of cultural vandalism and intellectual strangulation by the "Gang of Four" and China is sending more Peking Opera troupes abroad. It is my belief that this traditional Chinese theatrical form will eventually find its way to more stages in various parts of the world.

A GUIDE TO PEKING OPERA*

1. THE TYPES OF ROLES

In Peking Opera there are four main types of roles: *sheng* (the male roles), *dan* (the female roles), *jing* (painted faces) and *chou* (clowns).

The *Sheng* (The Male Roles)

The male roles in Peking Opera with the exception of painted-face characters are collectively known as *sheng*. Aged and bearded male characters are designated as "old" or *lao sheng*, while youthful male characters are known as "youthful" or *xiao sheng*. All who specialize in diction and singing are termed "civilian" or *wen sheng*; those skilled in acrobatics and military action are known as "military" or *wu sheng*. In the singing of a *wen sheng*, the most important consideration is that all high and low notes be sung in the best of style, and a thorough mastery of vocal technique is necessary, because, in the opera, the types of singing are exceedingly numerous. A *lao sheng*, often the role of a scholar, official, man of gentility or retired general must be proficient in conventional stage technique. In his enunciation, he must be fastidiously correct, while in acting, he must possess grace, dignity and distinction; above all, he must not overdo his part. The *wu sheng* specializes in bodily posturing and in conventional stage-fighting; the movements of his hands and feet must be clean-cut and his manner of expression good. In contrast to the *lao sheng*, the *xiao sheng*

---

* Based largely on the useful account given in the pamphlet *The Pacific Coast Tour of Mei Lanfang* compiled and edited by Ernest K. Moy in 1930.

does not wear a beard and should be a refined and cultured young man. He recites and sings in a high-pitched, semi-falsetto as an indication of his youthfulness.

The *Dan* (The Female Roles)

The general term in Peking Opera for all female roles is *dan*. Formerly, the term *dan* meant female impersonator, because in the old, feudal China men and women were forbidden to play on the same stage under the necessity to maintain a strict separation of one sex from the other, and so young men were trained to play the female roles. After the fall of the Qing dynasty (1644-1911), however, the old order of things began to change. Nowadays, female roles are generally played by actresses, though a few female impersonators (like Zhang Junqiu and Mei Baojiu, Mei Lanfang's youngest son) still occasionally appear on the stage.

The term *dan* is sub-divided into five types: *qing yi*, *hua dan*, *cai dan*, *lao dan* and *wu dan*. The following are their main distinctions:

The *qing yi* is the type representing the good matron, faithful wife, or filial daughter. In this type singing is greatly stressed and no fighting and acrobatics are required. Characteristic actions often give clues to the type. The *qing yi* is most properly behaved. Her footsteps are even and carefully taken while in walking the feet are kept close to the ground. The hands, always in a graceful and dignified position, are often crossed. On entering or withdrawing, the head is slightly inclined forward; on leaving the stage the right sleeve is often elevated.

The *hua dan* or "flower" *dan*, is the role for a vivacious maiden or a woman of questionable character, great emphasis being placed on the acting. Most charming are her ways, as she sways with airy grace on the stage, her left hand on her waist and her right hand holding a red handkerchief. Her every movement vibrates with life, from the suggestive glance of her eyes to the turn of her head.

Xiao sheng

Lao sheng

Qing yi

Hua dan

Lao dan

Jing

Wen chou

Wu chou

The *cai dan*, in point of liveliness, is akin to the *hua dan*. But she is comical lowly, and detestable. Her long strides are full of energy; her eyes roll in diabolical mischievousness.

The *wu dan* or military type is strong, beautiful, and vibrant with action, for she must enter the fray of battle and give exhibitions of acrobatics of the most difficult character. Sharp and bright are her eyes.

The type for an old woman or *lao dan* is the most realistic. With lowered head and stooped shoulders she totters across the stage. Sometimes she walks with a long staff for support. She is gentle and motherly. Her eyes mirror the tired expression of old age.

In singing, the voice of the *qing yi* is clear, and "pointed" with an inclination to be weak rather than robust. The voice of the *lao dan* is even, full, and patterned after that of an old woman. The *hua dan*, who relies on her skill in acting, may possess a voice of only average quality, although many have good voices.

The *Jing* (Painted Faces)

The actors of *jing* roles are required to paint their faces to a high degree, for which reason they are often called *hua lian* (painted face). They must be coarse and heavily built and possess voices that are rich and robust, while their movements must be dignified. The *jing* roles too are divided into "civilian" or *wen jing* and "military" or *wu jing*. A *wu jing* must be a master of boxing gymnastics and conventional military movements.

Actors playing *jing* commonly paint their faces in various styles that range from a single colour to bewildering combinations and figures. Many of the colours have a specific meaning. For instance, a predominance of red indicates that the person is courageous, faithful and virtuous; much black indicates a fierce and coarse nature; blue denotes cruelty while white symbolizes treachery. Green, blue, lavender and red combined have no deep significance.

The *Chou* (Clowns)

The general term for clowns is *chou*. Women clowns are called *chou dan,* while the men clowns are divided into *wen chou* (civilian clowns) and *wu chou* (warrior clowns). The whole group paint their noses powder-white, with a few black lines to show that they are clowns. Although other lines may, at times, be added to the face, the most common design is the butterfly.

The clown's main task is to win laughs from the audience; therefore, his lines must be especially well enunciated, sparkling with wit. If he displays military actions, they must be humorous in nature.

2. SINGING AND DECLAMATION

When a Peking Opera actor, especially an actor playing the role of *sheng*, comes upon the stage, he sometimes delivers what is termed the prologue, and perhaps poetry also, as well as the lines of a couplet. These distinctive practices on entering and exiting are characteristics which set classical Chinese drama apart from that of any other nation. The stage speech is invariably marked by a special cadence and rhythm and so differs, in a marked degree, from that of everyday life.

The Prologue (*Yin zi*)

When an actor makes his entrance, the first words he utters are what is technically known as the "prologue", which literally "introduces" the play. There is, during the recitation, a distinct rhythm; but there is no musical accompaniment (even not using the wooden clapper). A prologue generally fulfils one of the following functions: it may narrate roughly the entire action of the play, serve as an introduction to the character in question, or explain the act immediately to follow.

Poetry While Seated (*Zuo chang shi*)

After the prologue has been delivered, the actor, seating himself, usually recites four lines of poetry, technically termed "poetry that opens the play". In idea and construction, this same practice, also called "poetry while seated", bears a close resemblance to the prologue. Its origin comes from the style of the Chinese novel, in which there are always at the opening of the work a few lines which outline the entire theme.

Announcing One's Name (*Tong ming*)

After an actor has recited his four lines of poetry, he never fails to tell the audience the name of the character he plays, or if he does not recite poetry, he usually announces his name immediately after the delivery of the prologue.

Lines That Actually Open the Play (*Ding chang bai*)

The technical term *bai* means "to speak". An actor, having gone on stage and recited his prologue and poetic lines and having announced his name, proceeds to deliver what is termed the *ding chang bai,* in which he gives a detailed account of the character he plays, his family, or the story of the opera, often of the immediate act or episode at hand.

After an actor has delivered his *ding chang bai*, the actual play begins to unfold. While the actor recites the prologue, poetry, and the *ding chang bai*, he is mirroring the general mood of the action or the theme of the play. In subsequent acts, the same introduction may be effected once again, because some of the episodes were too far apart, and because changes of costume sometimes led to the audience forgetting the names of the various characters.

The Aside (*Bei gong*)

The aside may be described as words uttered to oneself in the presence of two or three others on the stage to reveal one's emotion or secrets to the audience. If the character is suddenly overcome by emotion, he naturally expresses himself by means of facial expression or pantomime; if the emotion is so complex that neither facial expression nor pantomime can make the meaning clear, then he lifts his sleeve, behind which he speaks or sings his explanation, or he may quickly step to one side of the stage, these actions making it clear that the others on the stage cannot hear what is being said. When a solitary actor sings or tells of his own affairs, the practice is also somewhat similar to the aside.

The "Call" or Signal for Music (*Jiao ban*)

After all the preliminary announcements have been made, the actor must prolong the last word he has uttered just before breaking into song. This is done by sustaining the last word, almost to a musical pitch, so that the musicians know by this signal (sometimes supported by such gestures as the waving of a sleeve) that the song is to follow at once and give them a chance to get their musical instruments ready for the accompaniment. Again, when the actor is about to conclude his song, he again prolongs the last word or two, so that the musicians will know that the singing is completed and will prepare to lay aside their instruments.

Singing (*Chang*)

It is common practice in Peking Opera when, during spoken lines, the emotions become raised to a high pitch, for the character to give vent to his feeling in song, as in moments of sudden fear, anger, grief or ecstasy. Again, there are occasions when long dramatic passages must be repeated by the actors, which also serve as reason for a long aria. If one character asks another about a matter, of which the latter is ignorant but about which the audience has already been informed, there is a possibility of the audience's patience being tried by the tedious repetition. The reply, therefore, is set to music so that the actor may have the opportunity to explain the situation, but to embellish his tale with such musical beauty as to save the audience the monotonous repetition of the spoken word.

Couplets Recited Before Going Off the Stage
(*Xia chang dui lian*)

After an actor has played his part and is about to move off the stage, it is customary for him to recite four lines, namely two couplets, or if two or more people exit together, they may recite four lines of poetry. These recitations are supposed to conclude the act or scene in question. The origin of such peculiar practices can also be traced to the literary form of the old Chinese novel.

3. PANTOMIME AND ACTING

Every movement made by an actor in a Peking Opera is made in accordance with time-honoured convention, and so is somewhat different from the action of everyday life. An attempt will now be made to explain some of these stage conventions.

Making Entrance and Exit

In Western drama, before the curtain rises, the actors have usually already placed themselves in appropriate positions on the stage and action begins as soon as the curtain has been raised. Peking Opera, however, opens to an empty stage, on which the various characters make their appearance successively. Before their entrance, the audience will be treated to an orchestral selection. Most of the movements of the actors are made to definite musical setting. All actions, even the simple act of walking, must be done gracefully and to a well defined tempo, which may or may not be set to musical accompaniment. The tempo is determined by the musicians. When an actor makes his first appearance, it is highly important that his every movement be pleasing to the eye, while every action is dictated by inviolable rules. An actor, speaking or singing before making his exit, is required to leave unsaid a few words, which, with his body slightly turned towards the audience, he declaims or sings, walks off the stage, like a kind of parting shot. The exit must also be done to musical accompaniment.

Walking and Running

The highly conventional gait of the various role types has a logical origin. The coarse types walk with long strides, and so the *jing* (painted-face) role type takes steps that are technically termed "wide". Both scholars and officials invariably move about with marked grace and leisure; thus, the gait of the *sheng* is described as "round", "square", or "dexterous", while female characters or *dan* walk with short, swaying, mincing steps, described as "slow", "graceful", etc. But no matter which role type is on the stage, he must take his steps in accordance with a definite and defined tempo; in situations demanding quick movement, there is the "swift tempo", while for slow gait, there is "slow tempo", and never for a moment does an actor of any merit dare to depart from that set tempo.

Passing Through a Door

Whenever it is necessary for an actor to enter through a doorway, he merely indicates that he has done so by lifting one foot as if stepping over the door-bar; while female characters raise the hand to show that they are leaning against the wall for support, this being a means of revealing the delicate grace that is associated with the fair sex. It makes no difference whether one enters or exits by the front door, room door, or garden door, the pantomimic action is the same. The actor merely indicates that he has opened or closed a door; with both hands, he pushes the imaginary panels of the door, sliding them apart or drawing them together. In cases of knocking, bolting, or locking a door, these actions are also indicated by panto-mimic gestures.

Movements in General

The Peking Opera actors must give their undivided attention to every movement. Their actions must be not only good to look upon but must also be executed in strict tempo. The movements of the head, the body, the hands, feet and arms must be done in accordance with established convention. The movement of a finger, the glance of an eye, the lifting of a foot, all entail a vast amount of study and practice and these movements must always be pleasant to the eye and made to the strict tempo as directed by the percussion musical instruments.

One of the many examples might make the point clear, namely, one of the positions of the *dan's* (female character's) fingers. The index finger is bent back with great strength; the thumb and middle finger from a circle; the ring finger is bent so that the tip rests against the middle joint of the middle finger; while the little finger must be curved so that its tip rests against the middle of the ring finger. This is but one example of the innumerable conventional practices and movements required by performers of Peking Opera.

Sleeping

When sleeping the actor does so by supporting himself on one arm against a table. When a *chou* or clown sometimes sleeps sprawled on a chair, his head thrown back, and his mouth agape, it is understood that it is done in this way merely to win laughs from the audience.

The Art of Dancing

In Western drama, it is common to see dancing, unaccom-panied by singing, or vice versa; in Peking Opera, however, dancing is accompanied by singing, as well as acting. Again, although Western musical drama has special regard for tempo, Peking Opera requires not only strict adherence to tempo but also that the dance movements must harmonize with the ideas of the written text, that is, the rhythm and action must be expressed in the musical score as well.

Miscellaneous Actions

It may be reiterated, in conclusion, that every movement on the Peking Opera stage is done in accordance with strict, time-honoured conventions. For example, when a male character laughs, he does so openly but a female character must conceal her mouth with her sleeve. In weeping, both men and women wipe away their tears with their sleeves; to express worry, the character frowns while moving his hand about; in meditation, the breast is stroked with a circular motion of the hand, the index finger being pointed to the temple, while to show bashfulness, the sleeve is raised before the face. Women cover their faces more completely than male characters in order to emphasize the innate modesty of their sex. In anger, the foot is stamped, the breast pounded. When one wishes to motion a person away, the hand is waved aside or the sleeve is flourished in outward motion, while to signal a person to come forward the hand is waved up and down just as Westerners wave farewell! To show fear, the body is turned aside, away from the source of fear.

4. COSTUMES

In the vernacular of Peking Opera, wearing apparel is generally termed *xing tou*, and is designed according to strict convention. The following are the more important garments worn.

The Ceremonial Robe

The ceremonial robe (*mang*) has a soft, kerchief-like collar, its large, overlapping front being buttoned from the collar, down under the arm and down the side, also inner, literally, "water sleeves" (*shui xiu*), which are long, flimsy, trailing silken inner sleeves, attached to the ordinary sleeves and hanging a few feet below the waistline, almost touching the ground. The body of the robe is satin, embroidered with dragons, while the lower border is decorated with representations of sea-waves. This is the most important garment for official attire, and is worn in audience with the Son of Heaven (the emperor) at official gatherings, at formal ceremonies, banquets, etc., or on any occasion of the first importance. The colours indicate the rank of the wearer, for example, imperial yellow for the emperor and the crown prince, incense-brown or white for senior officials, red or blue for upright persons, and black for coarse mannered or treacherous natures. On important festive occasions, even the warriors wear the ceremonial

Ceremonial robe (*mang*)

robe. The ceremonial robe worn by women, while in general like that worn by men, is somewhat shorter.

The Official Robe

The official robe (*guan yi*) is, in general, like the robe just described. It is because, prior to the Ming dynasty (1368-1644), only royalty and officials of the highest rank could wear the ceremonial robe, while officials of middle and lower ranks were obliged to wear the official robe. Official robes may be red, blue or black, the rank of the official being graded in the order of colour just mentioned. Attached to the front and back of the official robe are embroidered squares.

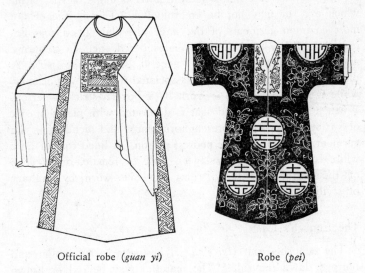

Official robe (*guan yi*)   Robe (*pei*)

The Robe

The robe, known as the *pei*, has a large collar and buttons down the front, with long inner sleeves, reaching almost to the knees. The garment is of satin, with various decorations, the flowers being sewn on whole or in scattered blossoms or broken branches. There is also robe without embroidery. Being an important garment, it is worn in ordinary banquet scenes or at official trials. In colour and manner of wearing, this robe is similar to the ceremonial robe. People of advanced age wear only blue or incense-brown, while those of middle age wear blue and youth red. The robe worn by female characters is similar to that worn by male characters.

The Lined Coat

The lined coat known as the *zhe zi* has a large collar and buttons under the arm, with inner sleeves and reaches to the feet. A woman's lined coat is somewhat shorter than a man's. The garment may be designated as soft or stiff, the former being of soft silk, while the latter is made of stiff satin, which may or may not be embroidered. This is one of the most common garments of the stage, the plain lined coat being more widely used than the embroidered one. In colouring and manner of wearing, it is in general like the robe (*pei*). A plain blue lined coat is usually associated with a young scholar, while a plain black one is worn by a poverty-stricken person. When a plain black lined coat is decorated with pieces of silk of various colours to represent torn places and mending in the garment, it is worn by the poorest person. A lined coat of pure white is worn by aged villagers, male or female, or by gods of the earth, etc. Lined coats may be worn by military or civilian characters.

The Eunuch's Coat

The eunuch's coat (*tai jian yi*) has a large soft collar and buttons down the side. The material may be red or brown silk, the whole having wide borders of black or blue. The waist may or may not be decorated or embroidered. The coat, reaching to the feet, has inner sleeves.

The Jade Belt

The jade belt (*yu dai*) is considered a very important article in an actor's wardrobe. To match a ceremonial or official robe, the jade belt is worn about the waist, this being the vogue previous to the Ming dynasty. The actual belt is made of stiff material which is studded with pieces of jade. That worn on the stage is almost an exact replica of the real one.

Jade belt (*yu dai*)

The Skirt

The skirt (*qun*) is worn exclusively by female characters. An official skirt is pleated and embroidered, but a common skirt is without decoration of any kind. Skirts of present day style only have four panels. When a skirt is fastened well above the waist, it is an indication that the wearer is a poor woman in travelling garb, which is supposed to be disarranged.

Jacket and Trousers

Old stage traditions, at least, did not permit women to show their trousers, but now for a century the vivacious character type, known as the *hua dan*, has always worn jacket and trousers (*ku ao*), doing away with the skirt. The jacket has a small collar and buttons down the side with string-fasteners, having plain sleeves, without the inner sleeves, the garment being about half the length of the body. Women wear such costumes on ordinary occasions only; on formal and festive occasions, they don the robe (*pei*).

The Sleeveless Coat

The sleeveless coat (*kan jian*) is worn by maid-servants only and is made of silk that may or may not be embroidered, and may or may not be bordered with other material. There are two sizes: the long type goes down to the knees while the short one reaches barely to the waist.

The Palace Garment

The palace garment (*gong yi*) is worn by princesses, daughters of aristocratic families or celestial beings, never by women of humble birth. Thus, the garment is called the palace robe. It is made of embroidered silk, having silken sashes, as well as inner sleeves; and is about knee-length.

The Tasselled Cape

The "cloud" shawl-like covering (*yun jian*) is worn over the ceremonial robe or official robe of an empress, a princess or a palace woman. It is circular in shape, and embellished with tassels and embroidery.

The Armour

The armour (*kai kao*) is the most important garment in a stage warrior's wardrobe, and is worn while in public service or when going into battle; but when in audience with the emperor, reviewing soldiers, or on festive occasions, a ceremonial robe must be worn on top of it. Its colour scheme and manner of wearing are similar to those of the ceremonial robe. An old general of distinction wears brown armour, while a youthful warrior wears white or pink. The "armour" is made of silk, embroidered back and front, and has narrow sleeves. Panels, designed to look like armour, are added to the sides, while at the breast is the so-called "heart-protecting mirror". Embroidered representations of tiger heads are attached at the waist and near the shoulders, all these details being patterned closely after ancient battle dress. The stage costume differs in its more elaborate decoration and embroidery. With the exception of the many hanging streamers, or sashes, male and female warrior costumes are alike.

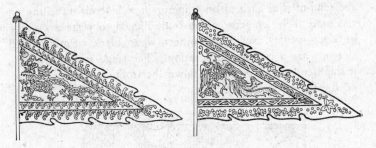

Military flags (*kao qi*)

The Military Flags

The military flags (*kao qi*) are the flags worn on a warrior's back when he enters the fray. The origin of these flags grew from their actual use by a general, who, when issuing orders in the thick of battle, gave one of his subordinates a flag to serve as a warrant. On one side of the flag were marks of identity. Every general took with him one or two flags to be used in cases of emergency. The flags now attached to a general's armour still retain the old idea of field orders, but the fact that there are four flags is due to a desire for beautiful effect. The flags (those with a dragon design are for a male role, while the phoenix-designed ones are for female role), triangular in form, are made of silk and embroidered with flowers or dragons. Their colour should be the same as that of the warrior's robe, that is white flags for a white robe, black for a black one, etc.

The "Horseback" Jacket

The "horseback" jacket (*ma gua*) was a garment still worn on top of the gown in everyday life, and was indispensable in China on formal occasions until the late forties. Invariably of black silk, the jacket buttons down the front and reaches a bit below the waistline. On the stage, the garment may be

the semi-official garb of an emperor or a general, travelling on
the road. The emperor alone is privileged to wear a *ma gua*
of deep yellow, while all others wear black. Embroidered
dragons are a common decoration. The stage *ma gua*, having
a small collar and buttoning down the front, was also introduced during the late Qing dynasty.

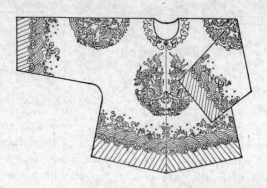

Horseback jacket (*ma gua*)

Headgear and Footwear

The hat, helmet and shoes, worn in Peking Opera, have
been designed from a combination of the styles that prevailed
during the Tang (618-907), Song (960-1279), Yuan (1279-1368),
and Ming (1368-1644) dynasties, and bear a very close resemblance to the originals although those used on the stage are
somewhat more elaborate.

The Helmet or Crown

The helmet (*kui*) or crown (*guan*) is the most important hat
of officialdom, only the emperor and high military officials being entitled to it. The hat of the emperor differs from all
others, in that it represents royalty. Tassels hang from the
sides. While the hat worn by military officials is somewhat
like that of the emperor's, the form varies according to the rank

of the person in question. For instance, an insurgent chief may sport a hat that is shaped only a trifle differently from that of the emperor.

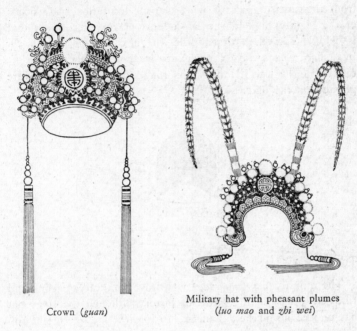

Crown (*guan*)

Military hat with pheasant plumes
(*luo mao* and *zhi wei*)

The Phoenix Hat

The phoenix hat (*feng guan*) is worn exclusively by women on formal occasions, and only empresses, princesses and women of high official families are privileged to wear such headgear, which consists of a framework, thickly studded with pearls and jade, with tassels suspended from the sides, while other tassels cover the forehead.

The Gauze Hat

The gauze hat (*sha mao*), also for officials, is worn exclusively by civil dignitaries when waiting on the emperor, attending public trials, festivities or banquets. Its form is very much like that used in real life in ancient times; low in front, high at the back, and black in colour. There extend horizontally from the sides a pair of wing-shaped decorations. Officials of the highest rank may wear a long, narrow decoration that is slightly curved in the middle, the next in rank may wear oval shaped ones, a rank lower may wear round ones, while the official of the lowest rank wears round decorations, which are pointed on the outer sides.

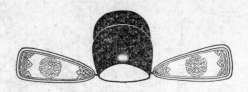

Gauze hat (*sha mao*)

The Military Hat

The military hat (*luo mao*) is worn by military persons and finds its origin in the pages of history although the stage hat has undergone marked changes. In form, it is large at the top and small near the head, while its six sides are richly embroidered and decorated with pearls and jade, its top being adorned with fluffy silken balls of various colours. This lavish display has for its sole purpose the pleasing of the eye.

The Pheasant Plumes

Sometimes two long pheasant plumes (*zhi wei*) are seen fluttering from an actor's headgear, the longest specimens being as much as six or seven feet in length. These feathers used to indicate that the wearer was from a minority nationality, or was an insurgent chief. As time passed, because of their striking beauty, pheasant plumes were also worn by other stage characters of the military type.

Shoes and Boots

On the traditional Chinese stage, actors wear boots with the exception of those playing the parts of women, poor scholars, labourers and farmers. While stage footwear is generally similar to that worn in everyday life, the soles of the former are made much thicker in order to give the actor additional height. Women wear shoes that are usually embroidered, while warriors' boots are embroidered and thin soled. The embroidery is merely to please the eye.

Beards and Moustaches

Since the ancients of China prized most of all a long beard, it came about that actors wore long beards made of horse hair. Although, at first, stage beards were not so long, they gradually increased in length. Varying through shades of white and black, the beard indicates the age of the wearer. Red or blue beards are worn by heroes of the greenwood, people of questionable character, masters of black magic, or supernatural beings. A full beard, which covers the mouth, indicates that the person is both wealthy and heroic. A tripart beard (a beard divided into

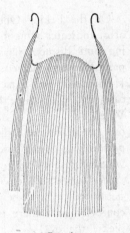

Beard

three parts) shows that the wearer is a person of culture and refinement. The short moustache, only an inch in length, indicates a crude and unrefined person.

The various types of stage beards are too numerous to be considered in detail. Briefly, it may be said that moustaches, pointing upward, reveal a crafty nature, while those drooping downward indicate an uncouth person, while some beards are worn merely to win laughs from the spectators.

5. STAGE PROPERTIES AND SYMBOLISM

Since in Peking Opera every situation, every object, must be abstract in nature and often symbolical, pure realism is invariably shunned and realistic stage properties are not favoured. Every object on the stage is fashioned according to strict convention. Sometimes, a common object may be symbolized, for example, an oar may represent a boat. This may be made clear by the following examples.

The Horse Whip

On the Peking Opera stage, the holding of a whip by an actor indicates symbolically that he is on a horse. Both mounting and dismounting are represented by strict conventional pantomimic movements. If the actor has already dismounted from the unseen horse, he may still hold the whip, but in that case, the whip must be allowed to hang at the rider's side. When he is about to fasten a horse to a post or tree, he needs only to place the whip on the ground or hand it to another person who is supposed to lead the animal away. A brown whip represents a brown horse; black, white, or reddish whips stand for horses of corresponding colour. When a whip is decorated with a bewildering variety of colours, it must be confessed that there is no such horse, but merely a desire to please the eye!

The Duster

The symbol of greatest refinement and the most highly treasured object throughout the long centuries of Chinese history was the duster made of horsehair. The literati, while conversing, delighted in fingering it; thus, in Peking Opera only the most exalted persons may hold a duster, like gods, demi-gods, bodhisattvas, Buddhist monks, Taoist priests, wanderers, recluses, celestial beings, and spirits of various

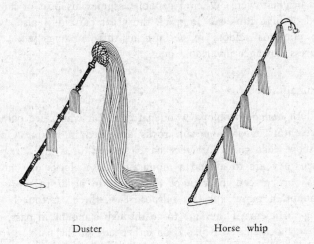

Duster   Horse whip

orders. Sometimes, however, a maid-servant may use one to
dust the furniture.

The "Wind" Flags

Four black flags, called wind flags (*feng qi*), are carried and
waved about by four attendants to show the blowing of a
great wind.

The "Water" Flags

Four flags with sea billows painted on a white surface, called "water" flags (*shui qi*), are used to represent ocean waves,
when a character leaps into a river and is rescued. These flags
are carried by four attendants.

The Great Curtain

The great curtain (*da zhang zi*) is a large embroidered
curtain, which may be used for many settings, most of them
being associated with women, for example, a bed, a canopy,

or a bright tower. When a general assumes his post or an official of high rank sits in state, the great curtain is also used. The emperor seldom makes use of this hanging, while the empress dowager invariably does.

Mountain Rocks

Cloth nailed to oblong wooden frames on which are painted representations of mountain rocks are used in Peking Opera to show that the characters have arrived in a hilly region. When they are to ascend a mountain, these blocks of "mountains" are placed in front of the actors in order to represent a mountain range, for this purpose two, three, or four blocks being sufficient; if they are to go through a mountain pass, one or two blocks may be placed on either side of the path in front of the travellers to represent the rocky formations that tower on either side.

The Table

The table represents many similar things, for example, a teapoy, a dining table, a judge's desk, an altar, etc., while the acts of going from lower to higher levels, as in the ascent of a mountain, or the scaling of a wall, may also be effected by the use of a table. When in use, the table may be placed in the usual position, or on its side, or in any position appropriate for the scene it is to be used in. There is no fixed rule for such placing.

The Chair

The chair (yi zi) is the most common object used for sitting on, yet the manner in which a chair is placed on the stage makes a decided difference. If the actor is seated in a palace, at an official gathering, or while reading or writing, the chair is placed behind the table and is then called "a chair inside" (nei zhang yi zi). If he is making preparations to receive guests, relatives or others for a quiet chat, the chair is placed in front of the table and is called "a chair outside" (*wai zhang yi zi*). There are, however, certain important occasions when a chair is placed behind the table. There are hair-splitting distinctions as to the manner of placing "a chair outside". For example, parents are seated in the centre, the place of honour, while the children take seats at the sides. Host and guest of equal rank sit on either side of a table in the centre of the stage, those of lower rank seating themselves farther away from the centre. On some occasions, women sit on the right and men on the left, the latter being the side of honour. If a father and a mother are seated, the daughter unfailingly takes the seat to the right. The manner of seating just described is also followed in daily life. If, however, an actor is supposed to be sitting on the ground, on rocks, or in any other unconventional position, the chair is placed on its side to show the situation, this being called "chair on its side" (*dao yi*). If a female character must climb to a higher place, she uses a chair to represent the climb. Although at times a male character may use a chair for the same purpose, he usually prefers a table. Again, two or three chairs placed together may represent a bed, a cloak or large covering being placed over the whole to complete the representation.

The Umbrella

The umbrella is commonly used in the Orient. An umbrella is held from behind, over the heads of the emperor and empress to protect them from sun and rain whenever they go outdoors. When officials conduct their business in the open, they also use the umbrella, while the fairies include pretty umbrellas in their train in order to appeal to the audience's sense of beauty. Umbrellas are made of silk, plain or embroidered, and the handles may be straight or curved, but are always long. The curved handles give the character more prestige than the straight ones.

The Ivory Tablet

The ivory tablet (*hu*) was used by officials, civil and military, in and prior to the Ming dynasty, as a mark of respect to the reigning house. In Peking Opera, when an official is in audience with the emperor, he must hold the tablet, which is usually made of ivory and is a foot or more in length and two inches wide, being narrow at the top and wide at the bottom.

Military Weapons

All military weapons used on the stage, such as lances, swords, guns, etc., are made of wood, and are careful imitations of the real articles although they may differ in size. Since stage regulations do not permit the use of real weapons, wooden ones are used instead.

6.   MUSICAL INSTRUMENTS

In musical drama the world over, it is customary for instruments to accompany the voice; in Peking Opera, apart from vocal accompaniment, orchestral instruments play interpolated passages, technically known as "passing the door" (*guo men*), for example, an actor has then completed the singing of a phrase, when the instruments play a few additional measures, thus giving the singer a pause and an opportunity to rest.

A general description of instruments follows:

The Clapper

The clapper (*ban*) is the main instrument used in a Peking Opera orchestra for beating time. While musicians of a Western orchestra "watch time" as directed by the conductor with the baton, Chinese instrumentalists "listen to time" as indicated by the sound of the clapper. The clapper is made of three pieces of wood of the hardest variety, two of them being fastened together side by side, while the other piece, tied at one end with a cord to the others, is, when keeping time, manipulated by one hand in such fashion as to hit against the other two with a loud resonant sound, castanets-style.

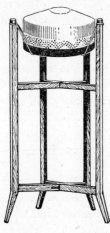

Small drum (*xiao gu*)   Clapper (*ban*)

The Small Drum

Although, in the music of Peking Opera, it is necessary to listen to the clapper, which maintains the tempo, yet at times the sound of the other music is so loud that the clapper cannot be heard. To avoid possible confusion, the small drum (*xiao gu*) is used, for its sound is much louder than that of the clapper. When cymbals and similar instruments are used, the small drum not only helps to keep time, but also creates flourishes which delight the ear. The small drum is made of heavy circles of wood, over which thick pigskin is stretched.

The Big Drum

The big drum is used mainly to assist in creating battleground effects. It is made of a wooden frame, over which cowhide is drawn.

The Fiddle

The fiddle used in Peking Opera is known as *jing hu* and is the most important bowed stringed instrument used for vocal accompaniment. Its sound box is made of bamboo, one end of which is covered with snake skin, while a bow is drawn between two strings to produce the sound. The fiddle is also called *hu qin* (the *hu* fiddle), because it originally came from the northern and western tribes known as the Hu people, from whom it derived the name *hu qin*. In course of time, however, the instrument has been modified and altered greatly.

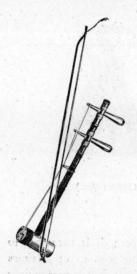

Fiddle (*jing hu*)

The Second Fiddle

The second fiddle (*er hu*), also a stringed instrument for vocal accompaniment, possesses tones that are somewhat lower than those of the *jing hu,* and is used to support the latter. It is also constructed of a wooden frame, over the end of which snake skin is stretched, its two strings being about one foot five inches in length.

The Four-Stringed Fiddle

The four-stringed fiddle (*si hu*), another instrument for vocal accompaniment, is similar in construction to the second fiddle, the only difference being that it has four strings instead of two.

The Moon Mandolin

The moon mandolin (*yue qin*), so called because of its round body, is an important plucked stringed instrument used for vocal accompaniment, and is to support the fiddle (*jing hu*). The instrument consists of a piece of round wood, with four strings, which are shorter than those of the fiddle (*jing hu*), being about five or six inches in length.

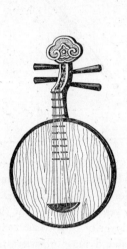 

Moon mandolin (*yue qin*)   Four-stringed lute (*pi pa*)

The Four-Stringed Lute

The pear-shaped four-stringed lute, known as *pi pa*, is also an important plucked stringed instrument. It has a mellow and extremely refined tone and it is widely used in traditional Chinese music.

The Three-Stringed Lute

The *xian zi* is another plucked stringed instrument that is commonly used in vocal accompaniment to assist the *jing hu*. It is constructed of circular pieces of hard wood, over which snake skin is stretched. It has three strings of about three feet in length, and possesses a slight overtone.

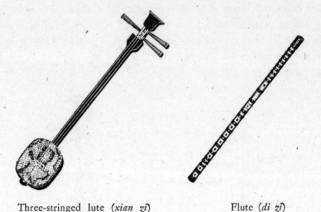

Three-stringed lute (*xian zi*)   Flute (*di zi*)

The Flute

The flute (*di zi*), also an instrument for vocal accompaniment, is made of a bamboo tube pierced with eight holes, and held parallel to the mouth when played. It is somewhat similar to the Western flute. It has a thin layer of rush tissue covering its second hole which produces a sound most pleasant to the ear.

The Reed Organ

The reed organ (*sheng*), also an instrument for vocal accompaniment, may be classified in the same family as the flute (*di zi*). While all other traditional instruments in China are single-toned, the *sheng* alone produces harmony. It is constructed of more than ten pieces of bamboo, each of which contains a hole, the entire number being fastened to a frame. The sound, produced by blowing, is weak but delightful to the ear.

The Chinese Clarionet

The Chinese clarionet (*suo na*), though customarily used as a solo instrument, may sometimes be used for vocal accompaniment. It is made of a piece of wood, pierced with eight holes. At the upper end there is a piece of rush tissue, attached to the mouthpiece, producing a loud sound when blown. At the lower end, there is a brass sound-magnifier. The Chinese clarionet is similar to its Indian and Turkish counterparts.

The Gong

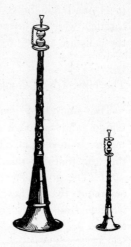

Chinese clarionet (*suo na*)

The gong (*luo*) is an entirely auxiliary instrument and is beaten when a musical passage is to begin or just about to close. When an actor first comes upon the stage, or is about to depart, or is executing pantomimic gestures, the gong is commonly used.

The Cymbals

The cymbals (*nao*), similar to those of a Western orchestra, are used after the fashion of the gong; they also are constructed of brass.

The Small Gong

The small gong (*xiao luo*) is similar to the large gong, and is beaten alternately with the larger instrument. It is used most when a *dan* (female character) steps upon the stage for the first time. While similar to the large gong in construction, the small gong is only six or seven inches in diameter.

The Bell

The bell is used exclusively to aid in keeping time, while additional tappings on the same are done to delight the ear.

It is made of brass and is cup-shaped with a hole bored through which a string is passed for hanging. When in use, the bells are clashed together.

The Nine-Toned Gong

The nine-toned gong (*jiu yin luo*) is played to restricted tempo, and although used in conjunction with other instruments, is never played when an actor sings, for it is believed that the tones of this instrument blur the tones of the human voice. The gong is made of nine circular pieces of brass, each of about two inches in diameter which are hung inside a wooden frame; they are hit with a small wooden stick in strict tempo.

Nine-toned gong (*jiu yin luo*)

SYNOPSES OF 25 PEKING OPERAS

THE ORPHAN OF THE ZHAOS

During the Spring and Autumn Period (770-476 B.C.), Zhao Dun, a minister of the State of Jin, was at variance with Tu Angu, a treacherous court official. Using his influence with the sovereign, Tu made a raid on Zhao's house, which took a toll of over three hundred. The only survivor, was Zhao's grandson, who was born of the sister of the sovereign in the palace. Even this orphan was not to go with impunity. The whole story of the opera centres around him.

Cheng Ying, a retainer of Zhao Dun, enters the palace in disguise as a doctor and smuggles out the orphan in a medical kit-bag. This was, however, discovered by Han Jue, a general, who has been sent by Tu Angu to guard the palace. Han Jue is a man of integrity. Being sympathetic with Zhao and his family and moved by Cheng Ying's brave deed, Han gives Cheng Ying a free passage, and then takes his own life.

In order to kill the orphan, Tu Angu cruelly orders all infants in the state between one and six months to be put to death. Under a plan jointly mapped out by Cheng Ying and Gongsun Chujiu, a close friend of Zhao Dun's, these infants, including the orphan of Zhao, are saved by sacrificing the lives of Gongsun and Cheng Ying's son. Later the orphan grows up under the care of Cheng Ying and eventually avenges himself on the enemy.

The story first appeared in the *Historical Records* by the great historian Sima Qian of the Western Han dynasty (206 B.C.-23 A.D.) and was adapted into a drama by the noted dramatist Ji Junxiang of the Yuan dynasty in the early 14th century. Since then, the drama has been popular for over six hundred years.

In the middle of the 18th century Joseph Marie de Premare, a missionary, translated it into French and published it in the *Description de la Chine*, which found its way into Europe. Voltaire in his commentary appraised the "Orphan of the Zhaos", although a work of the 14th century, as excelling those of French dramatists of his time. Among the adaptations made of the drama in European countries in the 18th century were the following: "The Orphan of China" (1758) by Arthur Murphy of Britain; "Eroe Chinese" (circa 1748) by Metastasio of Italy and "L'Orphelin de la Chine" (1755) by Voltaire himself. The drama has also been staged in Ireland and the United States.

THE GENERAL AND THE MINISTER ARE RECONCILED

The story of this opera is based on the accounts given in "Lian Po and Lin Xiangru" from Sima Qian's the *Historical Records*.

During the Warring States Period (475-221 B.C.), King Zhaoxiang of the State of Qin, adopting his counsellor Zhang Yi's tactic of befriending the distant states while striking at the neighbouring ones, frustrated the strategist Su Qin's plan of uniting the six states of Qi, Chu, Yan, Han, Zhao and Wei against the State of Qin. After sabotaging the unity of the six states, Qin intends to annex Zhao by tricking her into exchanging her rare treasure, the Heshi jade, for 15 cities of Qin, thus finding an excuse to attack if she should refuse. King Huiwen of the State of Zhao charges Lin Xiangru with the mission of delivering the jade to Qin, seeing how the land lay, and acting accordingly. Arriving at Qin and having found out that the offer is nothing but a fraud, Lin immediately has the jade taken back to Zhao. Then, at the ceremony of presenting the jade he exposed the trick of the King of Qin. Threatened with death, he shows no fear, but walks straight towards the boiling cauldron. The Qin king is compelled to release him.

Not reconciled to his failure, the King of Qin asks the Zhao king to a meeting at the border so as to browbeat him. While making full military preparations, the King of Zhao goes in the company of Lin Xiangru. At a banquet, the Qin king made the Zhao king play a lute in order to disgrace him. Lin Xiangru embarrasses the Qin king by making him strike a pottery jar. So the Qin king is frustrated a second time.

Lin has been a low-ranking official under the chief of Royal household Miao Xian. After these two events he is promoted several times until he finally becomes prime minister. But General Lian Po, who has accomplished many military feats, is unhappy about this. When Lin is made prime minister, the entire people of Zhao rejoice and celebrate, and court officials invite him to banquets. Lian Po, however, repeatedly provokes him on the streets. Although Lin is forbearing and conciliatory, he and the general fail to keep on good terms. When Qin instigates Qi to fight Zhao, the country is in danger of being attacked from both sides. The King of Zhao asks Yu Qing to mediate between Lin and Lian. Lin tells Yu Qing that the discord between the general and the prime minister of Zhao is just what Qin wants and so they must be reconciled. He says that he is willing to take the initiative to apologize to Lian Po if the latter would let him. On hearing this, Lian Po is greatly moved and feels deeply sorry. He immediately goes to Lin's house. Following the old Chinese custom, he takes off his hat and carries a birch on his back to ask for punishment from Lin. But the moment the two meet they kneel down in excitement and throw their arms around each other. Both pledge to unite and defend their country.

BEAUTY DEFIES TYRANNY

During the reign of the Second Emperor of the Qin dynasty (221-206 B.C.), there was a scheming prime minister named Zhao Gao, who had a beautiful daughter.

Zhao Gao tries by means of a marriage between his daughter Zhao Yanrong and the son of Kuang Hong, another minister, to win over the latter and form an alliance. Being an upright and honest official, Kuang Hong angers Zhao Gao because he refuses to lend support to his schemes.

The previous emperor Qin Shi Huang, the founder of the Qin dynasty, has given Kuang Hong a very precious sword called "Yu Zhou Feng" or the "Blade of the Heaven and Earth" (hence the Chinese title of this opera) as a token of his loyalty and now Zhao Gao sends his men to steal this sword and place it in the chamber of the Second Emperor.

Then Zhao insidiously suggests that Kuang Hong is disloyal to the emperor and has attempted to murder him. Consequently, the entire family of Kuang Hong, with the exception of Zhao Gao's son-in-law, are arrested and executed.

After the escape of her husband whom her father also tries to murder, Zhao Yanrong returns to her father's home.

One day the young emperor visits Zhao's home, and, noticing the beauty of Zhao Yanrong, orders her to be sent to the court to become one of his concubines. Zhao Gao is only too pleased to comply.

In desperation the beautiful daughter feigns madness, with the help of her deaf-mute maid-servant. So cleverly does she act the part of a mad woman that she finally manages to convince both her father and the emperor that she was really mad. In this way she avoids the fate assigned to her.

THE KING'S PARTING WITH HIS FAVOURITE

This opera is based on a story about the last moments of Xiang Yu, the King of Chu, who was defeated by Liu Bang, the King of Han, in their five-year struggle (206-202 B.C.) for national supremacy.

Yu Ji, the favourite of the King of Chu, enters singing that she has followed her royal spouse through many campaigns. Xiang Yu, the King of Chu, holds high a whip, which signifies that he is riding on his war horse Wuzhui. After the conventional pantomime of dismounting, he addresses Yu Ji who asks news of the day's battle. He tells her that after being entrapped in an ambush, he has suffered a reverse. Yu Ji consoles him, saying "Either victory or defeat, a soldier must meet. There is no need for despondence." They drink wine in order to forget their sorrows.

After drinking, the king and his beauty step behind the embroidered curtains which represent a bed. The beatings of the drum mark the passing of the night. Mindful of the king's problems, Yu Ji makes sure that he is asleep before she goes out into the moonlight to walk and think.

From the distant enemy camp are heard the songs of the State of Chu. Liu Bang, the King of Han, has his men sing the songs in order to weaken the morale of the Chu army.

Two soldiers are discussing the war situation and at once conclude that the songs are the evidence that the rival army have vanquished the people of their native state Chu and have been able to recruit men therefrom, so there are men singing Chu songs. The two Chu soldiers decide to support the rival leader.

Yu Ji, who overhears the conversation, is grief-stricken to learn that the soldiers intend to desert her royal spouse. When she has aroused the king, the distant song continues: "If we die on the battlefield, who will take care of our families?"

Wuzhui, the war horse, neighs mournfully outside the tent and is led in. The king addresses it as if bidding it farewell. Assuring her mate that his stronghold will stand firm until he has secured help, Yu Ji tries to persuade the king to keep up his spirits. Stricken with grief herself, she offers him wine while she sings and dances to boost morale. Secretly she wipes away her tears.

A messenger reports that the enemy are attacking them from all sides. Considering how to break through the siege, the king says to his favourite that they may never meet again, singing that if he should fall, it is because Heaven has decreed his end. The lady insists that even if he loses this battle, he can seek his fortune elsewhere and that he should not allow his concern for her safety to interfere.

The king requests her to take a carriage and go with him; otherwise he would not have the courage to fight his way out. This she refuses. Then he offers the idea that she go over to the rival ruler for safety. Yu Ji bravely refutes him, saying, "Your Majesty is wrong. A faithful minister will not serve two sovereigns; a virtuous woman will not marry twice. Since you are aiming at an empire, why should you lose heart for a woman? I beg of you the sword to end my life in return for your love and to relieve you from thinking of me." When the king refuses to give her the sword, she sings that she will not live on alone.

Diverting his attention, she seizes the sword and takes her own life.

ZHAOJUN CROSSING THE FRONTIER

This opera, adapted from a romance entitled *Tale of the Tomb*, describes how Wang Zhaojun, a court lady of the Emperor Yuandi of the Western Han dynasty (206 B.C.-23 A.D.), was forcibly sent to marry a chieftain of the Huns (a minority people living beyond the Great Wall) for the purpose of ensuring peace between the two peoples. It depicts what she saw and felt on the journey.

Threatened by the powerful Huns, the Emperor Yuandi is forced to marry off beautiful Wang Zhaojun to the ruler of the Huns in order to cement relations with him. Having said farewell to civil and military officials, Wang Zhaojun steps onto a carriage accompanied by Prince Wang Long, the emperor's brother-in-law, and leaves Chang'an, the capital, with extreme reluctance. She cherishes a profound love for her homeland and harbours a grudge against the emperor.

Before long, the carriage arrives at Yanmen, a pass on the frontier. The mountain road is so rugged that Wang Zhaojun, helped by a groom, has to mount a horse. The biting wind and the bizarre scenes of mysterious fog and scurrying clouds arouse nostalgia. Sitting in the saddle, she begins to play the lute as an accompaniment to her songs which express her love for her native country. In this mood, she reaches Fenguan Pass, whose exotic scenery again makes her miss her hometown and her parents. She wants to turn the horse and return to Chang'an. But on second thoughts, she realizes that she is now near the frontier and it would be hopeless to turn back. She continues on her journey.

THE EMPTY CITY RUSE

This is a story from the famous novel *The Romance of the Three Kingdoms*. It refers to an episode in the war between the Kingdoms of Shu (221-263) and Wei (220-265).

The Wei general, Sima Yi, sends his army to occupy the strategic places commanding the entrance to the important area of Hanzhong.

In view of Sima Yi's military movements, Zhuge Liang, the Shu strategist, ordered his army to come up and hold Jieting. But Commander Ma Su did not follow his order, lost the battle and fled the city. Consequently, Sima Yi occupied Jieting and his troops continued to advance on Xicheng, where Zhuge Liang stayed, but had no troops to cope with the enemy.

Zhuge Liang is warned by the old guards at the city gates of the imminent arrival of the enemy, but he reassures them. Then, mounting the city wall, he pretends to amuse himself, playing his lute, quaffing wine, and throwing the city gates wide open.

On his arrival, Sima Yi is puzzled by the sight and thinks that surely an ambush has been set, Zhuge Liang having a reputation for such tricks. So he retreats forty li and bides his time.

In the meantime Zhuge Liang manages to summon the forces of Zhao Yun, an ever victorious commander, to hold the fort for him.　Only then does Sima Yi realize that he has been outwitted, and beats a retreat.

Zhuge Liang later executes Ma Su, who has disobeyed orders at a critical moment, and at the same time he blames himself for having trusted a wrong man.

THE CROSSROADS

This is a rollicking, joyous piece of drama, based on an ancient Chinese folktale.

An upright and brave general, Jiao Zan, has been unjustly convicted and sentenced to exile.　His commanding officer is not convinced of his guilt, so he orders a young officer named Ren Tanghui to secretly follow and protect him.

Arriving at an inn situated at the junction of three roads, Jiao Zan and his custodial guards are received by the innkeeper — a kindhearted, jovial man named Liu Lihua, who finds the convict an honest and upright man.

Overhearing the guards plotting to murder Jiao Zan, Liu and his wife decide to intercede and save his life.　Later, Ren Tanghui arrives, but his repeated questions and the innkeeper's evasive answers make each suspect that the other is also involved in the plot to harm Jiao.

Ren puts up at the inn, and after he has fallen asleep Liu Lihua, the innkeeper, stealthily enters the room in the dark. (The stage, however, is brightly lit.)　His groping awakens Ren Tanghui and a fierce struggle ensues.　The comic hairbreadth misses hold the audience spellbound.

The confusion increases until at last the innkeeper's wife brings in a light, and Jiao, Ren and Liu recognize one another. Explanations are made all round, and the whole misunderstanding is cleared up.

THE WHITE SNAKE

Once there was a white snake who became immortal, living in the heavens.　She turned into a very beautiful girl, and came back to earth again. Here she met a blue snake, a lesser immortal being, who had also become a lovely maiden. She took Blue Snake as her maid-servant, and they set up house together in Hangzhou.

There they met a young man named Xu Xian, whom White Snake fell in love with and married.

Later, the scene changes to a city on the Changjiang (Yangtse) River where White Snake, now called Lady White, provides her husband with a medicine shop, and so uses her magical powers that all medicines become especially effective, and thus his business prospers exceedingly.

A Buddhist abbot now warns Xu Xian that his wife is actually a snake, and gives him a preparation for her to drink which will change her into her former, and real, self. But when Xu Xian sees her in her old form, he simply dies of fright. Then White Snake goes to heaven and, overcoming great difficulties, brings back a medicinal herb to restore him to life.

Far from being grateful, Xu Xian is even more scared of her than ever. He goes off to the Buddhist monastery by the Changjiang River where the abbot shelters him. White Snake comes and pleads with the abbot, but to no avail. Then in anger, she gathers together a great army of underwater creatures to attack the monastery.

Neither side wins this battle. The abbot tries to capture White Snake and fails. And she is unable to get her husband. The abbot realizes that one reason why his magical cunning has not enabled him to make his capture is that White Snake is pregnant. So he advises Xu Xian to go back and live with her until the child is born. On Xu's arrival, Blue Snake is about to attack him with her sword, but White Snake holds her back.

After the child is born, Xu Xian contrives, with the help of the abbot, to have White Snake revert again to her old form and be imprisoned under the Leifeng (Thunder Peak) Pagoda by West Lake in Hangzhou. However, Blue Snake later manages to destroy the Pagoda and rescues White Snake. The two return to heaven.

HAVOC IN HEAVEN

A very rare metal, which has hardened at the bottom of the river of the Milky Way, is carried away by the Monkey King. The Dragon King reports this to the Emperor of Heaven who dispatches Taibai Jinxing (God of the Planet Venus) to bring him in, trying to appease him by putting him in charge of the imperial horses. However, when the Monkey King hears of this, he gets into a great rage at the imperial horse stables, and on returning to his hideaway at Mount Huaguoshan (Mt. Flower and Fruit), he vows to fight the Imperial Palace by styling himself as Qitian Dasheng (The Godlike Sage). The Emperor of Heaven again dispatches Taibai Jinxing, this time inviting the Monkey King to an imperial party, planning to ambush him there. However, the Monkey King foils this plot, then gobbles up the sacred peaches, wine and other rare delicacies of the mountain hermits. He also eats up all the magic medicine, Jindan (the Golden Pills), which prevents both aging and death. But even the Monkey King occasionally lapses into carelessness: he gets bitten by one of the imperial dogs, and consequently is captured.

Furious, the Emperor of Heaven has the Monkey King thrown into a furnace, in order to burn him to death.

The Monkey King, however, has eaten some Jindan which give him renewed strength to break out of the furnace and return to Mount Huaguoshan.

The Emperor of Heaven, now in a rage, orders Li Tian Wang to lead all his soldiers in a great battle against the Monkey King, but they too are overcome by him.

YANDANG MOUNTAIN

When the curtain rises, amid the disheartening beating of drums and cymbals, a flurried and excited general with a painted face and a long black beard enters the stage. He is He Tianlong, a general of the Sui dynasty (581-618), who guards the Yandang area. Defeated by the peasant army led by Meng Haigong, he retreats to Yandang Mountain. When Meng Haigong and his men, in hot pursuit, lose track of the enemy, they decide to climb up the mountain and attack the enemy from behind.

Darkness has fallen when Meng Haigong goes downhill to begin their attack after reaching the summit. He encounters the enemy sentinels and they fight in the dark. He breaks through the blockade to confront He Tianlong's main forces. The sound of fighting reverberates through the mountain. Although the enemies push lumber and rocks down on the attackers, the brave insurgents finally defeat them and they are forced to escape into the lake.

Meng Haigong finds his way there and the two sides fight in the lake. He Tianlong's army is again defeated by the rebels.

He Tianlong then retreats to the Yanling Pass and tries to put up a stronghold there. Meng Haigong launches a powerful attack, shooting and killing the enemy guards with arrows. He climbs into the stronghold and wipes out the enemy.

By depicting the fierce fighting between the two armies, the opera extols of the courage and tenacity of the insurgents. Without words or singing it presents the characters and the story through acrobatic movements and dancing and mime. The magnificent, highly-skilled "fighting" offers artistic pleasure to the audience.

THE DRUNKEN BEAUTY

This opera deals with Yang Yuhuan (Lady Yang), the favourite of the Emperor Ming Huang of the Tang dynasty, whose long reign (713-755) marked the beginning of the decline of the empire.

One evening Yang Yuhuan, attended by her hand-maidens and the two eunuchs Gao and Pei, makes her way to the

Pavilion of a Hundred Flowers in the palace. She is joyous at the prospect of drinking with the emperor at the pavilion. She recites to the effect that although there are three thousand beauties in the palace, her lord has bestowed his favour on her alone.

After arriving at the pavilion, Yang learns to her astonishment that the emperor has gone to the Western Palace, the apartment of her rival, Mei, another of the emperor's concubines. She was deeply hurt. In attempting to conceal her burning jealousy and wounded pride, she consumes bowl after bowl of strong wine.

When the imperial concubine exits, the eunuchs move pots of flowers around to decorate the pavilion. (Here the pantomime and the words of the eunuchs alone suggest the existence of the unseen pots).

Yang re-enters with unsteady steps and sinks to her knees on hearing that the emperor has arrived. But the announcement proves to be wrong. She can no longer control the passions which the wine has aroused and sways about in a series of tottering dances.

When the eunuchs remind her that the hour is late, Yang Yuhuan, having once more expressed her regret at being unable to see the emperor, dolefully sings, "I return alone to the palace."

THE HEROINE SHE SAIHUA

This is an episode from *The Romance of the Yang Family Generals*, which depicts the wooing of Yang Jiye, the first senior general of the Yang family in the Song dynasty (960-1279), to She Saihua who subsequently became the dowager of the Yang family of generals.

The minister She Hong has a beautiful daughter, who is a crack shot and possesses great combat skill. Saihua is her name. One day when Saihua is hunting in the mountains she meets Yang Jiye, son of Yang Gun. After the cheerful meeting, they fall in love.

Yang Gun and another minister, Cui Zijian, have both asked She Hong for the hand of Saihua for their sons Yang Jiye and Cui Long respectively, when all three were serving as ministers at the court. Unfortunately She Hong has been so forgetful and muddleheaded as to have promised his beloved daughter Saihua to both the families and thus a serious dispute ensues.

Cui Zijian and the matchmaker Hu Yanping tries a ruse. They show to Saihua the portraits of the two young men who wish to marry her. The portrait of Yang Jiye is the epitome of ugliness while Cui Long is painted as a good-looking lad. But in reality the former is handsome and the latter ugly. Seeing these two portraits, Saihua is irritated and tears them to pieces. With reluctance, She Hong is obliged to follow the suggestion of Saihua's brother She Ying and invite the two youngsters to a contest. He promises to let the winner claim the bride.

During the contest, She Saihua herself joins the fighting and forces Cui Long to dismount. Then she pretends to be defeated by Yang Jiye. However, Cui Long does not admit defeat. Then, Cui Zijian leads his troops against She Hong, and Yang Gun also comes to reason with the Shes. Then the three families' quarrel turned to a tangled fighting. Taking advantage of the situation, Hu Yanping starts a rumour that She Ying has been killed by Yang Jiye. The impulsive She Saihua takes up arms against Yang to avenge her brother. Unable to resist Saihua's assault, Yang takes refuge in the Temple of Seven Stars.

Earlier, chased by Yang Gun, She Hong and Hu Yanping have run into the same temple to take refuge, disguising themselves as statues of gods. Yang Jiye wisely captures Saihua. And after clearing up their misunderstanding they take an oath before the supposed statues of gods to become engaged. Then She Hong and Hu Yanping throw off their disguises and step down. Hu Yanping apologizes to Yang and Saihua for having spread rumours and incited them to fight against each other. He volunteers to help arrange their marriage. She Hong

readily consents to his daughter's own choice of a husband.
So the two lovers get married and live happily together.

MU GUIYING TAKES COMMAND

Mu Guiying was a legendary heroine of *The Romance of the
Yang Family Generals* in the Song dynasty. In her youth she was
a woman military commander and rendered meritorious service
to the court. Nearly all the members of the Yang family who
were in military service gave their lives in the battles against
invaders. Yet, they did not enjoy the trust of the imperial
court. Later, Mu Guiying retired from the service and followed
her grandmother-in-law She Saihua to return to their home
village and live in seclusion.

The plot of the opera occurs some twenty years after Mu
Guiying's retirement when the country is again threatened with
invasion. An alarm is sounded from the frontier. The Song
emperor orders combat contests on the parade ground where
he will personally select his commanding officer. Yang Jinhua
and Yang Wenguang, the daughter and son of Mu Guiying,
take part in the contests. Yang Wenguang kills Wang Lun,
son of Wang Qiang, a treacherous court official, and secures the
commander's seal. Since the brother and sister are too young,
the emperor orders Mu Guiying to assume command. In-
fluenced by recollections of the past, Mu Guiying, at the sight
of the commander's seal, shows reluctance to direct the expedi-
tion. Through persuasion by the old lady She Saihua, she sets
aside her personal grievances, and proceeds to the front in defence of her country.

QIN XIANGLIAN, THE FORSAKEN WIFE

During the Song dynasty (960-1279), there once lived a poor
scholar named Chen Shimei in Junzhou (now Junxian of Hubei
Province). One year when the highest imperial examination

is being held, he goes to the capital to sit for the exam and wins the title "Zhuangyuan", the highest grade of scholar. Concealing the fact that he is already a married man and has a wife and children at home, he marries the emperor's sister.

The Junzhou area suffers from serious droughts for three successive years, and Chen Shimei's parents die of starvation. Qin Xianglian, Chen's first wife, sells a lock of her own hair and uses the money to bury them. Then she brings her son and daughter to the capital to look for her husband. Chen Shimei, greedy for high position and a luxurious life, pretends not to know his wife when he meets her. Driven to desperation, Qin stops Prime Minister Wang Yanling's sedan-chair in the street, accusing Chen Shimei. To find out the truth, the prime minister asks Qin to disguise herself as a street singer to play *pi pa* (a lute-like Chinese plucked string instrument) before Chen on his birthday, hoping that this would help him change his mind. But he has no intention of recognizing her. On the contrary, he sends his servant Han Qi to kill her and their children in an old temple. But on hearing her story, Han cannot bring himself to kill them. Unable to go back to his master, he ends his own life instead. Then Qin stops a most upright minister Bao Zheng's sedan-chair in the street, presenting her complaint against Chen Shimei. Bao invites Chen home and tries to persuade him to accept his wife and children. However, Chen turns a deaf ear. Counting on the fact that he is the emperor's brother-in-law, he makes a scene at court. As Bao is about to execute him, the empress dowager and the emperor's sister (Chen's second wife) come to intervene. Bao thinks he will not have the courage to see the wronged woman without putting Chen to death. To uphold justice, Bao, running the risk of losing his position, has Chen executed.

CALLING OFF THE FEAST

In the tenth century at the time of the Song dynasty, there was a successful politician named Kou Zhun.

Once, on the occasion of his birthday, he gives a sumptuous feast, and throughout the night the place is festooned with bright lights. There is much singing and dancing.

Then an old woman arrives, who, in Kou Zhun's childhood days, tended him and stood by him through all his difficulties. When she sees all the signs of dissipation and misuse of power, she feels sick at heart.

In the house of Kou Zhun, there is a servant named Chen Shan, who has broken some valuable household utensil and is to be heavily punished. The old woman has come to intercede for him.

As she comes through the halls and galleries, she slips and falls on the polished floor. This fall awakes in her a great anger and many memories. She then recounts to Kou Zhun the story of his mother's life, her bitter struggles and his own childhood.

Remorse fills the heart of Kou Zhun. He stops the feast, and remitted the punishment of the servant Chen Shan.

WILD BOAR FOREST

The plot for this piece of opera comes from the well-known Chinese novel *The Water Margin*. It was during the Northern Song dynasty (960-1127), towards the end of that dynasty's stay at Kaifeng, when many good and honest men were forced to join the rebels in the Liangshan Hills which stood by a margin of water.

An officer named Lin Chong makes a visit with his wife to a Buddhist temple. In the gardens of the temple, he meets a monk called Zhi Shen, for whom he cherishes an instant affection, and the two become sworn brothers.

Also visiting the temple is a young dandy, the son of the emperor's favourite minister Gao Qiu. Gao Qiu's son sees the pretty wife of Lin Chong and begins making advances to her. Then Lin Chong and Zhi Shen come up, and the monk promptly begins to beat the dandy for his effrontery. Lin Chong, knowing that he was the son of Gao Qiu, asks Zhi Shen to desist, and suggests that all should go their separate ways.

A scene from *Orphan of the Zhaos,* showing Cheng Ying (left) and Gongsun Chujiu.

A scene from *The General and the Minister Are Reconciled,* showing the general Lian Po apologizing to the minister Lin Xiangru.

A
C.
of
st
re
th
to

A scene from *The Crossroad*
showing a fight in the dar
between the innkeeper Li
Lihua (holding swords) an
the officer Ren Tanghui.

A s
Fore
has
er
mur

from *The Empty* . Before the arrival enemy troops, the Zhuge Liang the old guards at gates and tells them the gates open.

scene from *Calling Off Feast*. The old woman counts to Kou Zhun, a gh official, the story of childhood and reminds m not to forget his past fferings.

from *The Wild Boar* monk Zhi Shen (right) scued his sworn broth-ong (left) from being n the forest.

A scene from *Autumn River*. The Taoist nun Chen Miaochang has boarded a boat in order to pursue her lover. She is burning with anxiety, while the kindly old boatman teases on her.

A scene from *Romance of an Iron Bow*. Chen Xiuying, the daughter of the late garrison commander, draws the iron bow and then asks the young officer Kuang Zhong to try it. According to her father's will, she is to marry the man who is able to draw the bow.

However, Gao Qiu is already an enemy of Lin Chong's. When he learns of the beating of his son by Zhi Shen, he sends his men to make trouble for Lin. Lin has just bought a very fine sword and has it in his hand when Gao Qiu's men come after him, taking him into the big audience chamber. Then Gao Qiu appears, and accuses Lin Chong of an attempt to kill him. He then has Lin exiled under escort to Cangzhou, and secretly orders the guards to murder him on the way.

The road leads through Wild Boar Forest, an uninhabited place which the escorts think to be a suitable place to carry out Gao's order and murder Lin Chong. Just at this moment, however, Zhi Shen who has stealthily followed them from Kaifeng, appears unexpectedly on the scene and prevents the guards from carrying out their plan.

On his arrival at Cangzhou, Lin is sent to look after a big storehouse where fodder is being kept. When Gao Qiu hears of this, he orders his men to go to Cangzhou and set fire to the fodder at night and burn Lin Chong along with it. But early in the night there is a storm. It is bitterly cold. The storehouse in Lin's charge is blown down, so he goes to a temple for shelter. Just at that time the storehouse is set alight. Lin certainly would have been burned alive had he been in the storehouse. He is sipping some wine inside a temple room when he hears the would-be murderers come in, boasting of their deed.

Then Lin appears, throwing them all into confusion. He draws out his knife and stabs the leader of the band, just as Zhi Shen comes up again. Zhi Shen brings the bad news that, under the compulsion of Gao Qiu's son, Lin Chong's wife has committed suicide. So with his heart full of bitterness and hate, Lin goes with Zhi Shen into the hills by the water margin to join the rebels there.

THE FISHERMAN'S REVENGE

Along the shores of Taihu Lake there resides an obtrusive and influential retired minister, Ding by name. Seeing that the poor villagers take fishing as their livelihood, he begins to levy an unlawful fishing tax. The fishermen, though embittered, are powerless to resist.

There is an old fisherman named Xiao En who is living with his daughter Guiying. He has paid the fishing tax regularly. But due to a recent drought, no fish is caught and he is unable to pay the tax.

Ding sends his underlings to force payment. They arrive just when Xiao is having a drink with two friends on his fishing boat. The friends rebuke them and drive them away.

The underlings report the matter to their master and the latter at once communicates with the magistrate, asking him to have Xiao En arrested. Xiao goes to the magistrate to state his case but is reprimanded with flogging and ordered to tender apologies to Ding himself.

Xiao returns to the boat and plots with his daughter for revenge. The two go to Ding's house on the pretence of offering a big and precious pearl to Ding. The pearl is called Qingding Pearl (hence another title of this opera) which was given to Guiying by her fiancé as a token of their engagement.

After they are admitted into the inner yards of the house, the fisherman and his daughter kill the whole family of Ding and flee.

AUTUMN RIVER

Chen Miaochang, a young Taoist nun, dressed in a robe and holding a duster in her hand, comes in a hurry to the riverside and strains her eyes to search the turbulent waters.

Some time ago, she met Pan Pizheng, nephew of the abbess of the nunnery, and fell in love with him. On finding out about their secret meetings, the abbess immediately sent his nephew to sit for the imperial examination in Linan (then the capital of Southern Song dynasty and present-day Hangzhou). He was forced to leave without saying goodbye to his sweetheart.

Now, Chen Miaochang is very anxious when she fails to find her lover at the riverside.   He has already sailed down the river. As a boat comes along, she hails it in order to pursue her lover. The boatman, a humorous old man, learning that the girl is chasing after her lover, dawdles on purpose and demands an exorbitant sum from her.

The boat sets off across the rolling waters.   On the stage the actor and actress go through the movements of rising and falling with the waves as the boat skirts shallow waters and dangerous shoals and follows the sharp bends of the river.   The eager girl is burning with anxiety to catch up with her lover while the kindly old man plays jokes on her. But actually the old boatman has great sympathy for the girl and admires her boldness in seeking her love.   He oars hard in order that the girl may reunite with her lover as quick as possible.

The boat gains speed with the current.   It finally catches up with the young man, and the two boats sail along side by side.

Autumn River is an episode from the full-length opera *Romance of the Jade Hairpin*.

PICKING UP A JADE BRACELET

Widow Sun lives with her young and beautiful daughter Sun Yujiao who has a mild and bashful disposition.   They raise chickens to make a living.   One day, when her mother is away from home, Sun Yujiao is doing some needlework in her doorway.   A young man, Fu Peng, passes by and approaches her on the pretext of buying chickens.   The two fall in love at first sight, but both are so embarrassed that they do not know how to express their love.

Fu Peng, when leaving, drops a jade bracelet on purpose as a sign of love.   Sun Yujiao picks it up trying not to be seen as she is overflowing with the happiness of her first love.   But she is seen by the wife of a neighbour. The neighbour's wife, with great humour, discloses the facts of the girl picking up the bracelet.   Deeply embarrassed, Sun fails to keep a good front, and she can do nothing but admit her love. The warm-hearted neighbour's wife gets an embroidered handkerchief from the girl and sends it to Fu as a return gift in order to show the girl's love.

Traditional Peking Opera mime, such as the opening of the chicken coop, the feeding of the chickens and the application of the needle and thread in embroidery work, reflect the everyday life of the characters in the opera.

CHUN XIANG UPSETS THE STUDY

Chun Xiang is a young maid-servant who attends her young mistress Du Liniang. The two of them receive lessons from a tutor everyday in the study of their home.

Chun Xiang is very mischievous, and leads the tutor such a dance with her tricks that finally in despair he announces he is unable to teach any more and makes preparations to leave the place.

Du Liniang now on the one hand uses all her persuasiveness to put the teacher into a good humour again, and on the other curbs Chun Xiang's high spirits so that the studies can proceed again.

THE FAIRY OF AZURE LAKE

The opera starts with Zhang Zhen, a young scholar who has just lost his parents, going to his future father-in-law, Jin Chong, for help. Jin, the prime minister, is reluctant to receive Zhang and tells him to live and study in a cottage by Azure Lake on the pretext that "the Jin family has not taken any man without an official title as a son-in-law for three generations". Cold shouldered in this way Zhang feels extremely miserable and lonely. All he can do for consolation is to sigh and talk about his misfortunes to the fish inhabiting the vast expanse of blue water.

His plight unexpectedly wins the compassion of a fairy carp who dwells in the palace of Azure Lake. Having taken the form of Mudan, Zhang Zhen's fiancée, Fairy Carp comes one moonlit night to meet the young man in order to comfort him.

On the eve of the Lantern Festival, when the real Mudan is enjoying the plum blossom in the garden, Zhang Zhen enters to greet her, mistaking her for the same girl with whom he met and conversed that other moonlit night. On learning that this poor scholar is her fiancé, snobbish Jin Mudan makes a great hullaboloo. Making this an excuse, her father drives the young man out of the mansion.

When tender, intelligent Fairy Carp hears what has happened, she traces and finds Zhang Zhen in the downtown district. She cleverly explains how the "misunderstanding just happened", and the two make it up. While they are looking at lanterns of all kinds, enjoying themselves, they are seen by Jin Chong who immediately takes them home. So there are two Mudans now in the mansion.

In order to identify the real Mudan, Jin invites Bao Zheng, a judge who is said to try human cases during daytime and hear cases in the nether world at night, to hear the case. But Fairy Carp also calls on her fellows for help. A tortoise turns itself into another Bao Zheng. So there are two Bao Zhengs. The sham Bao Zheng convinces and wins over the true Bao Zheng by reasoning with him. And Bao Zheng, not wanting to separate the lovers, leaves the case unsolved.

When Jin invites Sorcerer Zhang Tian Shi to arrest Fairy Carp, she, anticipating the impending separation from her lover, tells Zhang Zhen the truth. The kind-hearted young man, grateful for her true love, does not change his mind. Fairy Carp, loving him all the more, puts up a fight against the heavenly troops in order to protect Zhang. At this crucial moment, a Bodhisattva comes to their rescue and saves them. Fairy Carp decides to live with Zhang Zhen for better or worse. So she turns down the offer of going with the Bodhisattva to be elevated to the rank of a real goddess, and painfully sheds three of her golden scales to show that her decision is irrevocable.

SELLING WATER

A scholarly young man walks onto the stage.   His brows lock-
ed, he staggers along under a shoulder-pole trying hard to steady
the water buckets swinging at its ends.   Shyly, he cries, "Water!
Water for sale!" while sadly recalling the misfortune that has
befallen his family.   The young man is called Li Yangui.   His
father Li Shou, ex-vice-minister of war, has been thrown into
jail on a trumped-up charge, and all his property confiscated.
Li Yangui and his mother can no longer afford to live in the
capital.   They have moved to Suzhou and make a living by
selling water.

His betrothed, Huang Guiying, also lives in the same town.
Her fiancé's misfortune distresses her greatly.   She is wearing
out her days in woe.   She especially hates her father (a person
who plays up to those in power) for attempting to break off
her engagement with Li Yangui.

Meiying, Huang Guiying's maid, is a clever girl who shows
great understanding and concern for Guiying.   One day, she
persuades her mistress to take a walk in the garden.   The lively
Meiying sings and dances, handkerchief in hand, amid the flowers, reaching out for branches or bending down to touch the
flowers.   In her singing she makes smiles with the flowers: praising the lotus for its purity, the hibiscus for blooming side by
side, the autumn chrysanthemum for withstanding wind and
frost, and the winter plum for defying ice and snow.   Then they
ascend a pavilion to enjoy the scenery.   There they happen to
see the young man selling water.   The pitiful state her fiancé
is in makes Guiying weep.   The clever Meiying, on the pretext
of buying water, arranges for the two lovers to meet so that
they can have a heart-to-heart talk and reaffirm their love for
each other.   When they part, Guiying tells the young man to
meet Meiying in the garden that night so that Meiying can give
him some money for her.

Selling Water is an episode from the full-length opera *Fiery
Steed*.

DONATING A PEARL ON RAINBOW BRIDGE

When Nymph Sizhou and many other fairies sing and dance, enjoying themselves on one side of Rainbow Bridge, they meet Bei Yong, the son of the governer of Sizhou, who is out sightseeing. The Nymph invites him to the palace at the bottom of the river. They enjoy each other's company and soon become engaged. When the time comes to part, Nymph gives her treasure — a bright pearl — to Bei Yong and they reluctantly leave each other.

The governer is against this engagement. To break it, he burns incense, asking the Jade Emperor of Heaven to intervene. In order to punish Nymph who has broken heavenly laws and fallen in love with a human being, the Jade Emperor sends his warriors Nezha and God Erlang and some troops to subdue her.

To protect her own happiness, the dauntless Nymph wages battle against the vicious enemies. To uphold justice, all the sea animals come to help her. But overwhelmed by sheer force of numbers they are defeated in the first battle.

At this crucial moment, Bei Yong overcomes all obstacles and risks his life to rescue her by giving back to her the pearl. Once the pearl is in her hand, Nymph, her strength increased, turns tables on the enemies and overpowers God Erlang and his troops. The love between Bei Yong and Nymph, having stood severe tests, becomes deeper.

LADY MAGNOLIA

During the Ming dynasty (1368-1644) there was a young scholar named Wang Jinlong. When in Beijing as a candidate for the imperial examination, he met Su San, a beautiful girl of sixteen, in a singsong house. Wang Jinlong lavished thousands of taels of silver on her, and gave her a new name "Yu Tang Chun" or "Lady Magnolia".

After Wang Jinlong has spent all his money on Lady Magnolia, the keeper of the singsong house refuses to let him visit her any more. Then, she is sold to a man, who is later murdered by his wife, for which crime Su San is wrongly charged. The county magistrate receives a bribe from the murderer and sentences Su San to death.

Now Wang Jinlong is appointed Circuit Judge at Taiyuan, provincial capital of Shanxi, following his success in the examination. The case of Su San is brought up before him for review and he orders a retrial.

Su San is brought to the provincial capital by an old warder. On the way, the tender-hearted old warder takes off her cangue and chains, and she tells him all her suffering.

When the case comes up in court, Wang Jinlong nervously shows his feelings. One of the other judges, who has learned of his infatuation, plays some practical jokes on him, for a time obstructing him in his efforts to save her. In the end, however, the court pronounces her not guilty.

Su San and Wang Jinlong then get married.

ROMANCE OF AN IRON BOW

The late Taiyuan Garrison Commander Chen Long's wife and daughter, Chen Xiuying, earn a living by running a teahouse called "Heroes' Haunt". One day, a dandy named Shi Lun, the son of Taiyuan's General Commander Shi Xulong, learning that there is a beautiful girl in "Heroes' Haunt", comes to the teahouse under the pretext of drinking tea. There he tries to take liberties with Chen Xiuying and then asks her to marry him. But he is thrown out by the girl's mother. On her way to chase the dandy, the mother meets with Kuang Zhong, an officer under Shi Xulong, who persuades her not to run after the hooligan. She then invites him to tea. Seeing an iron bow hanging on the wall of the teahouse, the man inquires about its origin. When he learns that the bow has been left behind by the late garrison commander, he asks Xiuying to draw the bow. She, too, asks

him to try it.   Afterwards, they practise boxing and soon fall
in love. According to the will of the late garrison commander,
his daughter should marry the man who is able to draw the bow.
The girl's mother readily consents to her engagement to Kuang
and it is decided that the wedding will take place three days
later.

To lay hands on this girl, Shi Xulong and Shi Lun hatch up
a plot.   Shi Xulong orders Kuang Zhong to send a hundred
thousand taels of silver to the troops at a border town as soldiers'
pay.   At the same time, a confidant of the Shis' called Wu Yi,
disguised as a robber, is sent to waylay him.   Kuang Zhong
loses the silver and is exiled to Yunnan.   Then, Shi Lun again
comes to the "Heroes' Haunt" and presses for marriage.   The
mother pretends to give her consent and entertains the man with
wine.   When drunk, Shi Lun is made to tell the truth about
the conspiracy and the frame-up against Kuang Zhong.   Chen
Xiuying kills the villain, disguises herself as a man and, with
her mother, goes to see Wang Fugang, a good friend of Kuang
Zhong. On their way to the Taihang Mountain, they meet Guan
Yueying, the woman head of a stockaded village and Wang
Fugang's fiancée, though they have never met before.   Because
Xiuying introduces herself as Wang Fugang, Guan Yueying in-
vites them to her home up in the mountain.   Together with
Guan's father Guan Bo, they decide to start an uprising.   Chen
Xiuying considers this to be an opportunity to get her revenge.
Not long after, dressed in a white robe and silvery armour, she
leads troops to attack Taiyuan.   Shi Xulong comes out to fight
her.   To avenge Kuang Zhong, she kills him.   Then the im-
perial envoy, Lord Wang, sends Wang Fugang to square up with
Chen Xiuying, but he is defeated too.   Xiuying demands Kuang
Zhong come out to fight.   Lord Wang summons Kuang from
exile and sends him to deal with Xiuying.   Thus the two lovers
meet on the battleground and get reunited.   Wang Fugang and
Guang Yueying, too, get married.

INDEX

acrobatics 2, 61,

acting, style of 2; aesthetic value of 3; symbolism in 3; question of good or bad 26; techniques of Chinese traditional 27; pantomime and 74-77 *passim*

actors 18, 43; basic training of Peking Opera 3, 31, 61; female role 8; four great *dan* (female-role) 8; not to identify with the character played 16, 17, 20; to enter into the character 17; isolation from audience 20; transmutation of 21; *see also* names of individual actors

actresses 6, 22, 61, 67

aesthetic basis, of Chinese classical opera 35

alienation, effect of 20

All-Union Society for Cultural Relations with Foreign Countries (VOKS) 60

Anhui, dialect of 5; troupes from 8

announcing one's name (*tong ming*) 72

Antoine, André (playwright) 20

Arabic decoration 55

arias, folk 5; new 10; long 73

armour (*kai kao*) 82

Arnold, Julean (U.S. Commercial Attaché) 50

art, ambassador in 1, 59; a comprehensive performing 1, 2; fine 41; a folk 6, 65; true 42; and everyday life 23; revolutionary literature and 25; the essence of traditional Chinese 28; the keynote for Western 28; exotic 54; unrealistic 55

artistic perception 42, 43, 44

Asakusa 48

aside (*bei gong*) 72

Atkinson, Justin Brooks (dramatic critic) 54

Attic Theatres 55

Audience 3, 6, 20, 21, 22, 24, 46, 47, 52, 55, 73, 74, 91

Autumn River (Peking Opera) 116

Bao Zheng (character) 113, 119

Baroque school 15

Barrie, James (playwright) 65

beard, red, blue, full, tripart (costumes) 87

Beauty Defies Tyranny (Peking Opera) 9, 27, 33, 34, 37, 101

Beauty Xi Shi (Peking Opera) 10, 51

Beijing (Peking) 2; dialect 5; "Four Happiness Troupe" in 8

Bei Yong (character) 121

bell 97

origin of 2; requirements for and training of actors of 2, 31, 61; types of roles of 5, 66-71 *passim;* pantomime and acting of 3, 4, 74-77 *passim; see also* gestures; spoken part of 4, 5, 71, 72; singing part of 4, 5, 73; musical modes in 5; musical instruments of 4, 5, 92-98 *passim;* make-up and mask design of 7, 55, 70; costumes of 7, 77-87; scenery and stage properties of 3, 7, 88-92 *passim;* method of presentation of 6; salient features and inner characteristics of, *see* under traditional Chinese theatre; differences between Western drama and 3, 15, 16, 19, 21, 22, 24, 27-29 *passim,* 53, 54

Peking Union Medical College 63

Peony Pavilion, The (kun qu opera) 44

Pickford, Mary (film actress) 51

Piscator, Erwin (dramatist) 61

pheasant plumes *(zhi wei)* 86

phoenix hat *(feng guan)* 85

Picking Up a Jade Bracelet (Peking Opera) 117

pi pa (four-stringed lute) 4, 113

plasticity 16, 28

poems, dedicated to Mei Lanfang 9; by Tagore 64

poetry, Chinese 2; while seated *(zuo chang shi)* 72

post-Qing officialdom 2

Premare, Joseph Marie de 100

prologue *(yin zi)* 71

properties: *see* stage

Qi, State of 100, 101

Qi Baishi (painter) 11

Qin, the King of 100; the State of 100; the dynasty of 101; Second Emperor of 102; Shi Huang (founder of the Qin dynasty) 102

Qin Xianglian, the Forsaken Wife (Peking Opera) 112

Qing Court 2

qing yi (type of role) 5, 8, 31, 32, 40

Qitian Dasheng (character) 108

Radek, Karl (journalist) 60

Radlov, S. (dramatic critic) 61

Rainbow Pass (Peking Opera) 12, 51, 63

realism 28, 41, 56, 63; critical 20; dexterous 55; three great masters of 15, 18

realistic portrayal 24

recitation, Chinese 2

Red Snake and the Golden Pin, The (Peking Opera) 49

reed organ *(sheng)* 96

reforms, in make-up and costumes 10; of traditional theatre 23

Reinsch, Dr. Paul (U.S. Minister to China) 49

Renaissance 15

Ren Tanghui (character) 106

"rhyme" part, the 5

robe *(pei)* 79

Robeson, Eslanda Goode (Mrs. Paul Robeson) 65

Robeson, Paul 12, 65

roles, types of 5, 66-71 *passim; see also* under *sheng* (the male roles), *dan* (the female roles), *jing* (painted faces) and *chou* (clowns)

京剧与梅兰芳

吴祖光　黄佐临　梅紹武　等著

＊

新世界出版社出版（北京）
外文印刷厂印刷
中国国际图书贸易总公司发行
（中国国际书店）
北京399信箱
1981年第一版
1984年第二次印刷

编号：（英）1000